Baseball

AN ALL-STAR SPORTS BOOK

Baseball

Joe Archibald

Follett Publishing Company, Chicago

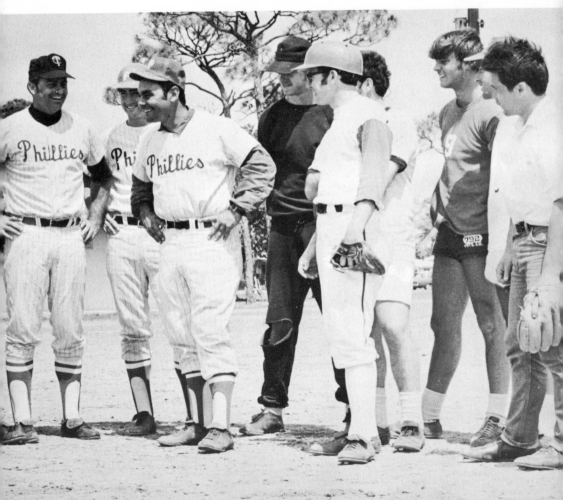

The author gratefully acknowledges the cooperation of Fred Ferreira, scout for the Philadelphia Phillies, who arranged for and permitted the use of the instructional photographs in this book; instructors Larry Brown, Dave McDonald, Johnny Ellis, Gene Michael, Danny Pfister, and Tim Valentine; and Mike Ferranti, Stuart Nathan, Tony Glassman, Charles Kanganis, Kevin Begner, Ralph Mastriani, Ricky Bernstein, and Javier Andino, who served as models.

Front Cover Photograph by Arnold Zann.
Back Cover Photograph by Howard Loth.
All other photographs by Larry Mailloux.

Diagrams on pages 43, 45, 55, and 114 are courtesy of Prentice-Hall, Inc., John W. Coombs, *Baseball*, Second Edition, Copyright © 1947. New renderings by Marc H. A. McIntosh.

Line drawings on pages 37, 51, 63, 74, 82, 92, and 109 are by Ray Naylor.

ISBN 0-695-40251-X Titan binding
ISBN 0-695-80251-8 Trade binding

Library of Congress Catalog Card Number: 71-159326

First Printing

CONTENTS

INTRODUCTION

Every year hundreds of youngsters work out at baseball clinics or instructional camps throughout the United States in the hopes that a big league scout will mark them as future stars and eventually sign them to a Class A or Class AA farm club contract. Only a handful will experience this thrill of a lifetime and for more than one reason.

To find out the reasons for the high dropout rate among so many hopefuls the author paid a visit to the baseball school-camp at Fort Lauderdale, Florida. The school is managed by Fred Ferreira, once a ballplayer in the Yankee chain, former scout for the San Diego Padres, and now southeastern scout for the Philadelphia Phillies of the National League. Along with the youngsters we found out what it takes to be a major leaguer, exploring several questions. First, how deep is a boy's desire to play baseball? Lack of a genuine love for the game or the right motivation have prevented countless youngsters from donning a big league uniform. Has he the willingness to learn? Does he "pocket his hustle" when his team is six runs behind? Is he a team player or is he only concerned with his individual performance?

Leon Hamilton, special assignment scout for the San Diego Padres, an instructor himself, puts it all in a nutshell. "When you get out there between those white foul lines, you have to forget that anything else exists outside of the ball game. There is no disgrace in losing, but never let a coach or manager catch you laughing about it. Play hard to win every minute, but play it clean, and always remember that moral character is as important as physical character."

The youngsters at Ferreira's school are taught the skills of the game of baseball during the off season by major leaguers, both active and retired, including Larry Brown, shortstop for the Oakland Athletics; Gene Michael of the New York Yankees; Dave McDonald, of the Class AAA Winnipeg Whips; Danny Pfister, once a pitcher for the Kansas City A's; Bob Feller, Hall of Famer and former Cleveland pitcher; and Johnny Ellis, first baseman for the New York Yankees.

During the past five years nearly thirty-five youngsters have been signed to big league farm club contracts under the guidance of Fred Ferreira and his staff; and twenty-seven others were helped in securing college scholarships. These boys had that deep desire to play, the willingness to practice, practice, practice until they had mastered the skills needed at their chosen positions on the diamond. They had the determination.

Youngsters today are offered modern training methods and major league development systems affording every one an equal opportunity to follow in the footsteps of a Ty Cobb, a Lou Gehrig or a Willie Mays.

It goes without saying that even though you show great promise as Little Leaguers or Babe Ruth Leaguers, you may not intend to play professional baseball as a career, but in the following pages the skills you will need to compete in grammer school, high school, or college baseball are explained in detail. Study them thoroughly and carefully and then go out and show those coaches that you belong on their baseball teams.

JOE ARCHIBALD

I'm sure that the young players will find BASEBALL by Joe Archibald very interesting and informative. Although natural ability is necessary to become a great player, learning and applying the fundamentals taught in this book will surely be beneficial to everyone.

LARRY BROWN
SHORTSTOP, OAKLAND A'S

BASEBALL by Joe Archibald is a complete and comprehensive guide to the fundamentals of playing each position on a baseball team and graphically explains all the proper defensive plays in every possible situation that arises during the course of a ball game, as well as offering instructions to individual players as far as offensive tactics are concerned. It is a book that should be read and studied by everyone having the desire to play the game whether it be on a sandlot, high school, college, or big league diamond.

FRED FERREIRA
PHILADELPHIA PHILLIES SCOUT

CHAPTER ONE

THE GAME OF BASEBALL

HISTORY The origin of the game of baseball, long considered the national pastime of the United States, is still very much a matter for conjecture. Archivists throughout the years have maintained that the sport evolved from the game of "rounders," played in England as early as 1830, and from modifications of similar games in the United States known as "One-Old-Cat" or "Two-Old-Cat," depending upon the number of bases used. Archaeologists believe that a crude form of baseball was played in ancient Egypt, but they have never discovered any relics closely resembling a bat or ball.

As early as 1839 Colonel Abner Doubleday, who for many years held the distinction of having invented baseball, established a set of playing rules; but the man generally recognized today as the father of American baseball is Alexander Cartwright, an amateur athlete and surveyor who umpired the first baseball game played under a set of rules in 1846 between the Knickerbocker Club and a picked team called the New York Club.

Players were not paid until the year 1869, when Harry Wright, a jeweler by trade, was paid $1200 to manage the Cincinnati Red Stockings. In 1867, William J. Cummings developed the curve ball, one of the most radical departures in pitching history. The National League was organized in 1876, the American League in 1901.

Black players began to get official recognition in 1947 when Jackie Robinson became the first black ballplayer to be brought up to the major leagues by Branch Rickey of the Brooklyn Dodgers. In 1971 the great black pitcher, Satchel Paige, was elected to the Hall of Fame.

All major league clubs have their farm systems where they develop young players. The Rookie League is the first step for hundreds of players that will strive to reach Class A ball. The next higher rung on the ladder is Class AA, and when a player is elevated to Class AAA he is knocking on the door of major league baseball. The farm system is good for the morale of all youngsters. It demonstrates to all those having talent that they will not be held in the minor leagues beyond a reasonable number of years.

The Little League, now called the cradle of professional baseball, was launched in 1939. It grew from one league, with three teams to twelve leagues in 1946, all in Pennsylvania, and by the year 1948 there were 94 leagues scattered over six states. Now there are nearly 3500 teams in Little League uniforms playing in 38 states and six foreign countries. Approximately 250,000 boys will be playing ball this year and the next under Little League rules and competent supervision.

Great changes have been made in the game since 1839 when in "Three-Old Cat," a batter could run to an outlying base and back to home plate as many times as he could before the ball was returned to the "catcher." The idea was to stay in as batsman as long as possible. Nine-inning baseball as we know it today, was not played until 1854.

Down through the years the game of baseball developed rapidly, and today just about every city, town, and hamlet in the United States fields a baseball team. The game's one-hundredth anniversary was celebrated in 1969.

THE RULES   The game of baseball is played between two teams of nine players on a side, each team striving to make more runs than the other in nine innings, which are the subdivisions of each game. One team takes its turn at bat while the other takes the field and attempts to put out three batters before any runs can be scored.

If the side that has been in the field at the end of the eighth inning is in possession of more runs than the side that has finished its time at bat in the first half of the ninth inning, the game is over, there being no reason for the leading team to go to bat again. If there is a tie at the end of nine innings the game is continued until one side or the other wins or until the game has to be called due to rain or because of a curfew that is in order in a certain community.

A player may be substituted for another at any time on either team, but a player, once out of the game, cannot return to it. To score a run a player must legally touch each base, beginning with first base, then second and third, to home plate again. If the side is put out before a player can score from any base he is "left on base."

The fielding side consists of the pitcher and catcher, often called the battery; first baseman, second baseman, third baseman and shortstop, called infielders; and left field, center field and right field, called the outfield.

The pitcher may throw overhand or underhand. Prior to 1875 the pitcher was obliged to deliver the ball with a forward toss only.

REGULATION BASEBALL DIAMOND The infield is a 90-foot square. The outfield is the area between the two foul lines formed by the extension of two sides of the square. The distance from home plate to the nearest fence, stand, or wall to either right field or left field should not be less than 300 feet and as much as 400 feet to center field. The infield should be graded so that the base lines are level with home plate with a gradual slope from

14

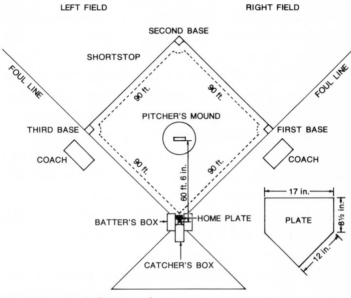

CENTER FIELD

LEFT FIELD   RIGHT FIELD

SECOND BASE

SHORTSTOP

FOUL LINE   FOUL LINE

90 ft.   90 ft.

PITCHER'S MOUND

THIRD BASE   FIRST BASE

COACH   COACH

90 ft.   90 ft.

60 ft. 6 in.

17 in.

8½ in.

BATTER'S BOX   HOME PLATE   PLATE

12 in.

CATCHER'S BOX

Regulation Baseball Diamond

the base lines up to the pitcher's mound which is 10 inches above the base line level.

The foul lines and all other playing lines indicated in the diagram by solid black lines should be marked with white lime, chalk, or any other white material. Home plate is a five-sided slab of whitened rubber. The front side measures 17 inches, the parallel sides 8½ inches, and the two sides that

15

are the extension of the base lines, 12 inches. The pitcher's plate is a rectangular slab of whitened rubber 24 inches long and 6 inches wide. The batsman's lines on either side of the plate are 6 feet long and 4 feet wide. The base bags should be 15 inches square and not more than 5 inches thick, and filled with soft material.

KEEPING SCORE Scoring a ball game whether you're at a game or watching it on television gives you a feeling of participation. The players on the field are numbered as follows: 1—Pitcher, 2—Catcher, 3—First Baseman, 4—Second Baseman, 5—Third Baseman, 6—Shortstop, 7—Left Fielder, 8—Center Fielder, 9—Right Fielder.

Many fans have their own system of scoring. Below are signs and numbers of one frequently used scoring system:

K2—Struck out, swinging. Kc—Called out on strikes. K2-3—Struck out, but catcher had to throw the runner out at first. K—Foul tip on third strike held by catcher.

BB—Base on balls. IBB—intentional walk to batsman. H by P—Batsman hit by pitcher. FC—Fielder's choice. On misplays on the part of the infielders, put down E-5, E-6, E-4, or E-3. Sac—Sacrifice bunt. SF—Sacrifice fly. SB—Stolen base. PB—Passed ball. T—Advanced on throw. WP—Wild pitch. X—Force Out.

When a fly ball is caught by the left fielder,

PO	A	E	Player	Pos	1	2	3	4	5	6	7	8	9	10	11	12	AB	R	H	RBI	SB
Team _ROYALS_																**Place** _BOSTON_					
3	0	0	HYSON	8	K2		FC<		KC/			6.3					4	0	0	0	0
3	3	0	KOLB	6	1.3	BB/				F2		5.3					3	0	0	0	0
2	0	0	WELDON	7	(F3)		(L7)/			(8)		(9)/					4	0	0	0	0
7	0	0	ZACH	3		BB 4-6	HR ◇		43/			K2					3	1	1	1	0
5	0	0	PIERRO	9	(F3)		K2			(9)		3-1					4	0	0	0	0
0	3	0	STANG	5	FC WP	6.3				D-LF<		S-LF					4	1	2	0	0
4	0	0	ALLMAN	2	8/		5.3/			(6)		S-LF L					4	0	1	0	0
3	1	0	SCHAUL	4		S-CF 6.4	KC			IBB/		S-LF/					3	0	2	1	0
			RUIZ	1		8F											0	0	0	0	0
0	1	0	BURCH	1		K2		K2		43/		6.3/					4	0	0	0	0
27	8	0	Time of Game _2:47_		0/0	0/0	0/1	1/0	0/0	0/0	0/0	0/0	1/0				33	2	6	2	0

The scorecard enables the viewer to record all the plays of the game in coded form. The columns are the daily totals. PO—Putouts; A—Assists; E—Errors; AB—At Bats; R—Runs Scored; H—Base Hits; RBI—Runs Batted In; SB—Stolen Bases.

put down the number 7 and circle it. Fly balls to the other two outfielders also are marked down according to their numbers. When the ball is lined out to the outfielders, add an L to the circled player's number. If fouled out to the outfield, put the letter F next to the fielder's number.

If a batter grounds out to shortstop, simply put down 6-3 in his square on the score card. If to the second baseman, 4-3, and if to the third baseman, 5-3. Double plays, with very few exceptions, are made by the infielders. Short to second to first would be marked down, 6-4-3; second to short to first, 4-6-3. When a runner is put out trying to steal, catcher to shortstop, put down AS, 2-6. AS means an attempt to steal.

Other signs are S-RF—Single to right field. D-LF—Double to left field. T-CF—Three-base hit to center field. HR-LF—Home run over that part of the fence. B-S-3B—Bunt single to third base. S-2B—Infield single to second base.

When a double play is made at first base, unassisted, put down the number 3 in the first baseman's square and circle it. If he threw to the shortstop or second baseman to complete the double play, then mark down either DP-3-6, or DP-3-4.

When a home run is hit, most scorers draw a small diamond under the signs, HR-CF, RF, or LF depending upon the spot where the ball sailed over the fence. Base advances may also be noted by drawing the diamond shape as far as the advance, with home plate in either the upper or lower part of the square.

In the diagram are the signs and numbers used by the majority of fans scoring the "Royals" half of a ball game against the "Bruins." The above symbols should enable you to follow the action, starting with the first inning, when Hyson strikes out.

BASEBALL TERMS

Appeal: The act of a fielder in claiming violation of the rules by the offensive team.

Around the Horn: A double play from third to

second to first when there is a runner on first base. This runner is forced at second and the batter is thrown out before he can reach first base.

Assist: You will be credited with an assist when you help a teammate make a play but do not make the actual putout yourself. A second baseman in fielding a ground ball throws to first and the baseman there gets credit for the out. The second baseman gets an assist.

Backstop: The catcher. Also a screen placed behind home plate to stop fouls from hitting the spectators.

Balk: A pitcher bluffing a throw to a base while standing on the pitcher's rubber is charged with a balk and runners on the bases are allowed to advance one base. You balk if you let the ball slip out of your glove when your foot is on the pitching slab, or do not come to a full stop when bringing your hands down from your pitching stretch.

Ball: Any pitch that misses the strike zone at home plate, and is not struck at by the batter. Four balls entitle the batter to first base.

Base on Balls: Also a walk; An award of first base to the batter when the pitcher throws him four pitches outside the strike zone.

Batter's Box: The place at home plate in which. the batter must stand during his time at bat. He must not step outside that box while hitting or he can be declared out.

Batting Average: To find out how good a hitter you are, divide the number of hits you make by the number of times you go to bat. If you make three hits in five times at bat you are hitting .600.

Batting Order: The lineup; the order in which the nine players on a team go up to bat. If one bats out of turn, he is out.

Bench: Where players sit, in uniform, when not playing on the field. Also refers to a team's substitutes or reserve players.

Blooper: A short fly ball that drops out of the reach of the fielders.

Box Score: A summary of a game printed in the newspapers giving the positions of the players, their at-bats, runs, hits, and runs batted in. Also included are the number of hits, bases on balls, and strike-outs turned in by the pitchers.

Breaking Pitch: A curve ball.

Bunt: A punch at the ball that should not send it too far from the plate and out of the reach of the infielders. Used to advance a baserunner at the cost of an out.

Change-Up: A pitcher giving the batter a slow ball after pitching him a fast ball. It generally finds the hitter off stride.

Choke Hitter: A batter who holds the bat far up on the handle and takes a short swing at the ball rather than trying to hit for distance.

Cleanup Hitter: The fourth man in the batting order, considered the best hitter on the team who can be relied upon to drive base runners in.

Control: A pitcher is said to have control if he

allows few bases on balls.

Count: The number of balls and strikes called on a batter by the umpire.

Cutoff Play: A throw from an outfielder to the plate that is cut off by an infielder who will try to cut down an advancing base runner when he sees there's no chance to catch a man running to the plate.

Dead Ball: A ball out of play due to a legal suspension of play.

Double: A two base hit.

Double Play: Putting two men out on the same play.

Earned Run: A run scored by a clean hit or forced in by a base on balls, charged to the pitcher. A run scored on an error is not charged to the pitcher.

Earned Run Average: To determine a pitcher's ERA divide the number of innings he pitched by 9, then divide that into the number of earned runs. 12 earned runs in 54 innings gives a pitcher a 2.00 average. (54 divided by 9 = 6; 12 divided by 6 = 2.00)

Fair Ball: One that is hit into fair territory inside the right and left field foul lines.

Fielder's Choice: The act of a fielder who, rather than throwing a grounder to first, throws to another base to retire a runner already on base.

Force Out: With a base runner on first, the next batter hits to the second baseman who throws to second to force the man running from first. The batter reaches first. No tag has to be made on a force out.

Force Play: A batter having to run to second when the batsman after him hits to the infield. Unless an error is made he is an easy out.

Foul Ball: A legally batted ball that lands in foul territory, that part of the field outside first and second base. It is a strike, unless caught on the fly, in which case it is an out.

Foul Tip: A batted ball that goes off the bat directly into the catcher's mitt. It is not a foul tip if the catcher drops the ball.

Grand Slam: A home run with the bases loaded.

Ground Rules: All ball parks are not of the same dimensions. Managers and umpires agree on certain ground rules affecting play during the course of a game.

Hit and Run: Used to avoid a double play. The base runner starts for second just as the ball leaves the pitcher's hand. The batter must swing at the ball and try to hit to right field.

Hitting to Wrong Field: A left handed "pull" hitter hitting the ball to left field and a right-handed batter hitting the ball into right field.

Hot Corner: Third Base.

Illegal Pitch: Any pitch delivered to the batter when the pitcher's pivot foot is not in contact with the pitching rubber.

Infield Fly Rule: If there are men on all bases before two outs are made, a batter who hits a fly ball which can be easily caught by normal effort is automatically out. Runners may proceed at their own risk.

Interference: Any effort on the part of the team at bat to obstruct, impede, or hinder any fielder attempting to make a play.

Jamming: A pitcher throwing the ball to the batter on the inside corner of the plate.

Keystone: Second base.

Leg Hitter: A batter that beats out a lot of infield hits due to his great running speed.

Meat Hand: The hand not wearing a glove or a mitt.

Mop-Up Man: The relief pitcher who pitches the last two or three innings.

Move to First: The pitcher's attempt to catch a runner off first base.

Nightcap: The second game of a double header.

On-Deck Circle: Where the players wait their turns at bat, halfway between the dugout and home plate.

Passed Ball: One that gets by a catcher, one he could have stopped.

Pepper: Warm-up game played at close range on the sidelines.

Pickoff: Catching a runner off base, most generally off first base.

Pitchout: A ball thrown wide of the plate by the pitcher when a runner on first seems about to steal second. It gives the catcher a chance for a quick throw to the second baseman.

Pull Hitter: A batter that hits balls just inside the foul lines. A left-handed batter "pulls" to right, the right-handed batter to left.

Putout: The act of retiring a base runner or a batter by a defensive player.

Relay: A ball thrown into the infield by an outfielder, the infielder "relaying" the ball to another fielder to try and cut down a runner trying to advance.

Rubber: The pitcher's plate.

Run Down: The attempt at tagging out a runner caught between bases.

Sacrifice: A play in which a batter "sacrifices" himself as an out to advance a base runner. He either hits a long fly ball to score a runner from third when there is only one man out or bunts.

Save: A relief pitcher is given a "save" when he preserves a ball game started by another pitcher.

Set Position: Pitcher's position when there are men on bases.

Scoring Position: Usually at second or third base. A single can score the man on second. A long fly to the outfield can score a man from third.

Sidearm: A pitch delivered below shoulder level, coming diagonally across the plate.

Sinker: A pitch that suddenly breaks below the batter's knees when it reaches the plate.

Slider: A pitch not more than ten years old. It has more speed than a curve and has some spin on it.

Squeeze Play: A play attempted by a team when it has a man on third and only one out. The batter is ordered to bunt and as he does, the runner on third breaks for the plate. This is the suicide squeeze. When the runner heads for the plate *after* the ball is bunted, it is called the safety squeeze.

Steal: When a base runner takes an extra base without being advanced by a hit, an error, or a base on balls.

Strike Zone: The pitcher must throw the ball no lower than the batter's knees or higher than his armpits and get it over either corner of the plate at the same time.

Swinging Out in Front: Hitting at a ball, particularly a slow ball, before it gets across the plate.

Switch Hitter: A batter who hits from both sides of the plate, batting right-handed against left-handed pitchers and left-handed against right-handed pitchers.

Tag Up: Base runners must touch the base they are on before advancing another base after a long fly ball is caught by an outfielder.

Take: A batter watching a good pitch go by without swinging at it, usually when he has a count of three balls and one strike.

Texas Leaguer: A short fly-ball that drops for a hit between the infield and the outfield, beyond reach of the fielders.

Total Bases: A batter is credited with one total base for a single, two for a double, three for a triple, and four for a home run. A batter who has hit a single, a double, and a home run has hit for seven total bases.

Triple: A three-base hit.

Triple Play: Putting three men out on the same play; and it cannot happen with fewer than two runners on base. This is one of the rarest plays in baseball. Ron Hansen, playing with the Washington Senators became the eighth man to make one unassisted, in July, 1968.

Waste Pitch: A pitch thrown intentionally wide of or over the plate when a pitcher has two strikes and no balls on the hitter, one he hopes the batter will swing at and strike out.

Wild Pitch: A ball thrown so far out of the strike zone that it cannot be handled by the catcher. It cannot be charged against the pitcher unless there is at least one runner on base who advances on the pitch.

CHAPTER TWO

EQUIPMENT

The regulation baseball, covered with two strips of white horsehide and stitched together should weigh no more than 5¼ ounces and measure not less than 9 nor more than 9¼ inches in circumference.

The bat should not be more than 2¾ inches in diameter at the thickest part and no more than 42 inches in length. Only 18 inches of the bat handle may be treated with any substance used to improve a batter's grip. Colored bats are not allowed.

The catcher may wear a mitt not more than 38 inches in circumference and not more than 5½ inches from top to bottom. It may be of any weight. He wears a padded chest protector with an attached neck guard, double-kneecap leg guards, and a leather and metal mask standardized by sporting goods companies and approved by league officials.

The first baseman's glove should not be more than 12 inches long from top to bottom and not more than 8 inches wide across the palm. The space between the thumb and the finger section should not exceed 4 inches at the top of the mitt and 3½ inches at the base of the thumb crotch. Any enlargement of this space is disallowed.

All the infielders and outfielders' gloves are also 12 inches long and 8 inches wide, the space between the thumb crotch and forefinger, not to exceed 4½ inches. The webbing of the gloves may be of standard leather or lacing and any enlargement of this space is illegal. The glove may be of any weight, but must be all one color.

All players on a team must wear uniforms identical in color, trim, and style. No part of a uniform shall include a pattern that suggests the shape of a baseball and no metal or reflecting objects may be worn. No player is allowed to wear frayed, ragged, or slit sleeves.

The purpose of the baseball uniform is not just a display of ornamentation; it was designed for *protection*. Care should be taken in the adjustment of the uniform to make certain that the sliding pads are in the right place to minimize the risks of sliding that often result in painful skin abrasions. The undershirt should cover the upper part of the body and extend well below the hips, and the supporter should be adjusted over the bottom of the undershirt to prevent it from slipping during play. The top shirt should reach at least halfway between the hips and the knees.

The inner socks and outer stockings should be brought up well over the knee-joints. If all the pads are properly in place, the player should be well protected from the waistline almost to the knees.

Take care of your baseball shoes and your glove. The best shoes are made of kangaroo leather. They can be kept soft and pliable with a waterproof oil. After every game, particularly after one that has been rainy, clean and oil them properly before placing them in your locker.

It goes without saying that baseball uniforms must be cleaned often, for soiled garments worn close to the body can cause serious infection. If you play baseball a lot during the summer, bear in mind that cleanliness is imperative. Get those under-clothes and socks into the family wash after each game or practice session. Athlete's foot can be very irritating and is highly contagious, so wear clogs into and out of the shower room.

The batting helmet should be worn when you go up to hit otherwise serious injury may result. Wearing the "hard hat" is now compulsory in the major leagues, and one should be worn even if you're only playing in a sandlot game. Hip pads should be worn to protect against "burns" sustained in sliding, and they should be tied over both the inner and the outer shirt.

Many batters today wear golf gloves with the fingers cut off to guard against blistering their hands, and some wear a shin guard to protect themselves against a leg injury from being hit by their own batted balls. This equipment is optional and legal.

CHAPTER THREE

PITCHING

With the possible exception of the catcher, the pitcher holds down the most difficult position on a baseball diamond, for besides throwing the ball he has to be alert to every offensive and defensive situation on the field. He needs physical stamina, an even temper, and plenty of courage.

As the starting pitcher you will be the center of attraction when you walk out to the mound and will realize that the outcome of the game, one way or the other, rides on your every pitch. Do you have good control today or will you take an early shower? The pressure is on you, but it should be gone after you get those first three batters out.

Before you assume your pitching position, always turn to make sure your fielders are ready. As you begin the windup, your pivot foot should be in contact with the pitching rubber, and your other foot upon the back edge of the rubber or directly behind it. The weight of your body is on the *back* foot. From this position you must commit yourself to the pitch without hesitation or you will be charged with a balk, allowing a runner or runners that might happen to be on base to advance to the next base. You are allowed to throw to any base occupied by a runner providing you step directly toward such a base before making your throw.

A recently established rule penalizes a pitcher who brings his pitching hand to his mouth before stepping off the mound. A ball is charged against him. This rule was made to guard against a pitcher that might be considering throwing a "moist" or "spitball," an illegal pitch that gives a ball an added spin or "break." A pitcher must deliver the ball to the batter twenty seconds after it has been thrown back to him by the catcher.

There are three ways to deliver a pitch: straight overhand, three-quarter overhand, and sidearm. The sidearm pitch is thrown shoulder-level, the ball coming diagonally across the plate, and very few pitchers use this delivery. You should hold the ball in the same position whether you intend to throw a fast ball, curve, or slow ball. You need to "hide" every pitch, holding the back of the glove directly toward the batter, the ball pushed well back into the webbing of the glove. Never let the opposing coach or hitter see your fingers or upper part of your wrist.

The ball is held so that the pitcher makes three contacts with the ball between the thumb and fingers and the three seams. Young pitchers make

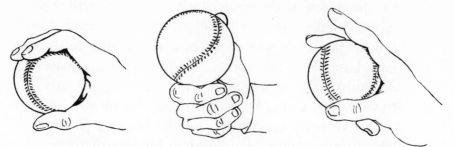

(left) Correct position for holding the ball for a fast ball or curve. For a fast ball, the wrist snaps forward and down, the ball rolling off the tips of the index and middle fingers. (middle) For a curve ball, the thumb is bent slightly, and the ball goes over the index finger as the wrist is turned. (right) For a change of pace or slow ball, the ball is gripped tightly in the curve formed by the index finger, thumb, and palm, and is thrown with a firm wrist.

the following mistakes:

1. Holding the ball *across* the seams near the tips of the fingers for a fast ball, then forcing the ball against the flesh between thumb and forefinger or holding it with the seams for a curve.

2. Holding the first and second fingers close together to throw a fast ball, then holding first and second fingers wide apart to deliver a curve ball.

3. Forcing the ball into the lower part of the hand with all fingers showing for a slow ball.

THE CURVE BALL The ball is gripped tightly with the middle finger regardless of the pressure that might be placed upon it by the forefinger. It is the twist given the ball that makes it curve. The ball must go over the forefinger as the wrist is turned.

Bob Feller shows the correct way to hold the ball.

The more the wrist is bent, the greater is the curve. The curve can be thrown half sidearm or overhand, the sidearm having no change in height as it goes to the plate. It does not dip down but breaks outward from the batter.

THE SLOW BALL   The pitcher holds the ball in the basic position. As it is about to leave his hand, it is relieved from the pressure of the first and second fingers, but is still gripped tightly by the thumb. The two fingers released, as the ball is delivered, point straight at the batsman. The ball is held against the upper part of the palm by the pressure of the thumb and if by chance the ball in leaving the pitcher's hand touches the fingers the ball will curve. The slow ball is usually pitched so

33

that the catcher receives it below or around the batter's knees.

THE FAST BALL   As in the basic grip, the index and middle fingers should grip the ball across the seams, with the ball of the thumb underneath. The ball should roll off the fingertips. The delivery is made overhand or three-quarter overhand. More often than not the fast ball is a pitcher's bread and butter if he mixes it with curves and slow balls. It is thrown with all the speed a pitcher possesses and sometimes tails away from a batter. This is called a "live" fast ball. Fast balls do not break. A pitcher simply tries to throw them past the batter.

THE FORK BALL   This pitch is a slow ball thrown with a little more speed and never should be thrown when there is a runner on base, for it will give that runner a chance to steal before the catcher can throw to a baseman. The ball is held tightly between the second joints of the first and second fingers which are spread wide apart. The tips of the fingers are bent slightly toward the palm of the hand. It leaves the hand without spin or rotation, and "floats" toward the plate.

Pitching coaches everywhere do not recommend that young pitchers experiment with freak deliveries, particularly the screwball, a pitch made famous by the immortal Christy Mathewson, who

Before delivering the ball, the pitcher faces the batter.

called it a "fadeaway." This pitch involves muscular movements of the wrist, forearm, and elbow contrary to nature's laws. The ball leaves the pitcher's hand between the second and third fingers and is pushed over the second finger by the thumb, giving it a spin and a downward movement, the catcher having to catch it well below his knees. To avoid serious arm injury, a pitcher should let the screwball alone.

Another unusual pitch is the knuckle ball, used by very few pitchers. Difficulty in controlling the pitch prevents its widespread use, and if catchers

35

had their way it would be outlawed altogether. If you want to try your luck with such a pitch, which does not cause any undue strain on a pitcher's arm, hold the ball with the thumb and have either the third or little finger pressing against the sides of the ball, the other fingers bent at the middle joints and resting on top of the ball. This pitch is almost impossible to perfect.

Despite your assortment of pitches they will be of little use to you unless you have that most important asset, control, the ability to keep getting the ball over the plate in the strike zone. There are several causes for lack of control. If you find yourself throwing too many high balls, it is apparent that you are not following through properly. Bend your back with every pitch; that is, follow through with your body motion and have your pitching hand almost touching the ground if you throw overhand. If you're a sidearmer, bring that pitching hand well around your body with your follow-through.

Over-striding means taking too long a step forward from your pitching position. Taking a stride of no more than a step toward the plate in a straight line with the plate will give you the correct follow-through.

There are two pitching positions, the wind-up and the stretch. With the bases empty the pitcher can take a full wind-up, raising his arms over his head before delivering the ball. With runners on

The pitcher's weight is on his rear foot before he begins the windup. He swings his arms over his head and shifts his weight from the back to the front foot. The leg nearest the batter is raised high and the pitching arm brought back. As his front foot and leg are thrown toward the batsman, his arm is brought forward. The rear foot leaves the pitching plate with a violent push as the ball is delivered with a snap of the wrist. After the ball is thrown, the body continues moving forward and around in the follow-through.

base the ball is held in the glove level with or just a little higher than his waistline and thrown from that position. From this pitching position he is able to throw to any base to put out a runner trying to advance. The stretch and the short wind-up are one and the same thing.

Even veteran pitchers make the mistake of not keeping their eyes on the catcher's target before they release the ball. Your catcher's mitt is the target, and you should keep your eyes on that mitt during the entire wind-up, rather than upon some imaginary target you pick for yourself. Most of the top-flight pitchers today advocate throwing the ball at a particular part of the catcher's body instead of aiming at parts of the plate. For example, if a batter is weak hitting high-pitched balls, you should aim your pitch at the shoulders of the catcher; and if a batter does not like inside pitches, you should throw to the shoulder of the catcher nearest the batsman.

A correct wind-up has a lot to do with your control. Bring your hands up. Your weight · is shifted from the back foot to the front foot, and your leg nearest the batter is lifted high. The ball is at its lowest level and your eye is on the catcher. You have turned your front shoulder as far as possible without obstructing your view of the batsman and the catcher as you come to your natural throwing position. Your body turns and your back foot leaves the pitching rubber with a hard thrust. As soon as the ball has left your hand, you should be in a terminating position with your back parallel to the pitching plate, enabling you to avoid being hit by a line drive, or go to either side of the mound to flag down grounders or swinging bunts.

Fatigue robs a pitcher of his control. To be a nine-inning pitcher, you must have strong arms and legs and plenty of wind. You owe it to yourself more than to your trainer or coach to keep in condition. Running strengthens your legs and builds up your wind. Chase fungoes—balls hit to the outfield by a practice bat called the fungo stick, one slightly flattened on the sides. Get into those pepper games. They will strengthen your back, for that is the part of the body you bend with every pitch. Run a lap or two around the ball park before practice starts. Neglect these important workouts and you will find yourself a bullpen pitcher, a "mop-up" man.

PITCHING STRATEGY An alert mind as well as a strong arm is needed on the pitching mound. A pitcher must always be aware of every defensive situation in which his whole team is involved.

When the opponents have runners on first and third, your catcher may signal for a pitch outside the strike zone, one that cannot be hit by the batter. It is called a waste ball or a pitch-out and puts the catcher into a correct throwing position if the base runners try to steal. The pitcher, after the ball leaves his hand, moves toward first base to cover that position, for the first baseman is trailing the runner toward second. The waste pitch must never be close enough to the batter to be hit!

Under certain conditions the pitcher is faced with the possibility of a squeeze play: when the batter at the plate signals to a runner on third that he is going to bunt the next pitch. One way to prevent the squeeze is to pitch the ball in close to the batter, or "brush" him back from the plate. There should be no thought in the pitcher's mind to hit the batter with the pitch.

When a left-handed hitter is up at the plate, and the base runner dashes for the plate just as the pitcher starts his wind-up, the ball should be pitched outside the plate so that the catcher can dive upon the runner attempting to score on the squeeze. If the catcher has given the sign for a curve ball in the same situation, the pitcher must keep the ball away from the batter, to the outside of the plate. Never ignore the catcher's sign for such a curve ball. If you throw a fast ball, he is not expecting it and is not ready for it. The result is generally a passed ball, a pitch that gets by the catcher and allows a run to score.

Think ahead when you're on the pitching mound; anticipate that the ball may be hit back to you. On slow-hit balls between the plate, the pitcher's box, and first base, you should yell, "I've got it," when you field the ball. If you are close to first base, throw to that base underhand, and throw hard. If you make the pick-up near home plate, near the foul line, throw to first base well inside the foul line so that you will not hit the runner with the ball. If the ball is hit beyond your reach between the mound and first base, the first baseman must leave his position to field the ball. You break quickly to first base to take the throw from the first baseman.

The safest way to handle that throw from the first baseman is to run about ten feet inside the foul line and take the throw while running along the base line, and tag the inside of the bag with your right foot. This avoids a collision with the base runner. This is one of the hardest plays a pitcher is called upon to make and you should work on it whenever your team is having batting practice.

The importance of back-up plays on the part of the pitcher cannot be stressed too highly. The moment a ball is hit to the outfield, he must quickly size up the situation, anticipate where the throw from an outfielder must be made, then break for the back-up position behind third base or home plate as the situation demands. To guard against having the ball bounce by him, a pitcher should station himself at least 30 feet behind the base or home plate. Never should he try to field the ball with one hand; he should get down on one knee and be ready to block with his body.

Before he throws to a batter a pitcher should

have his mind made up as to just what he is going to do in the event certain fielding situations arise. A golden rule for any pitcher should be: *Follow the ball. Back it up wherever it is thrown.*

Bear in mind that bases are stolen, eighty percent of the time, on the pitcher, not the catcher. The base runner studies your every arm and leg movement closely, and checks the time you take between pitches. Therefore you should never make a change in your motion when throwing to first base or to the batter at the plate. Vary your time between taking your pitching position and your deliveries to the plate. Count two, then pitch; count four, then pitch, and so on.

THE PITCHER AS A FIELDER A good fielding pitcher is the dream of all baseball managers. Bobby Shanz, the diminutive pitcher for both the old Philadelphia Athletics and New York Yankees was just about the greatest fielding pitcher of his era. He was as quick as a cat getting off the mound to field bunts and could throw accurately when completely off-balance. He always seemed to know what a certain opposing batter was going to do when runners were waiting to be advanced.

You must become adept at fielding bunts and backing up throws from your outfielders, and covering first base when that baseman is drawn off to field a ground ball the second baseman cannot reach. If you are in the right fielding position at the

42

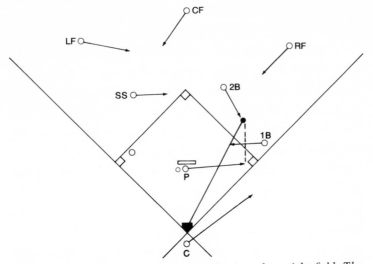

With one out, the batsman hits a grounder into short right field. The first baseman comes in to try and field the ball, but it gets by him, the second baseman moving in fast to pick up the ball and throw it to the pitcher covering first. Note the position of the outfielders and the catcher, the arrows indicating back-up positions in the event that the batsman tries to advance a base after a wild throw.

right time, you will be of tremendous help to your team. And you will help your own cause holding down the number of bases stolen by the other team. Too many stolen bases add up to earned runs scored against you, and a pitcher's earned run average is what keeps him in the major leagues.

When ground balls are hit to you, never toss the ball on the run to the first baseman, for many a run has scored and more than a few games lost when the ball has been tossed over the first baseman's head. A hard throw is more accurate; it gives the baseman time to recover if he happens to drop the ball.

To be a valuable "fifth" fielder, you need to put in hours of practice, working out with the first and third basemen on bunt coverage. Listen to your catcher when you are about to field a bunt. He will tell you what base to throw to, otherwise you are likely to "freeze" the ball and will still be holding it while the base runner reaches first. Remember, bare-handed pickups are not recommended unless you are a fielding wizard like Brooks Robinson of the Baltimore Orioles.

There are several basic fielding rules that you, as a pitcher, should fix firmly in your mind:

1. With a runner on second base and a base hit made to the outfield, you should position yourself in a direct line with the outfielder who is to throw into the catcher. If you are told to cut the throw off by the catcher, you take it quickly and throw to second base to cut down the batter trying to reach that base. If you hear the order, "Let it go!" by the catcher or any other infielder, step aside and let the catcher try to tag out the leading base runner at the plate.

2. If a fly ball is hit to the outfield with a runner on third base, you back up the plate.

3. With a runner on second base and a fly ball hit to the outfield, you must back up third base.

4. When a ball is hit to you and a runner stops

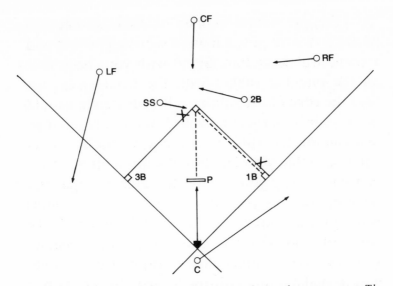

A hit-and-run play is called with a man on first and one man out. The batter hits a slow grounder to the pitcher who throws to second although he has no chance to put out the base runner, who has gotten a head start even as the batter had hit the ball. Both runners are safe. Note the movements of the catcher, the left fielder, and center fielder. They are all in the right positions to back up possible wild throws to any base. Had the pitcher made the correct play at first, there would have been two men out and only one runner on the bases.

between bases, rush toward him and get between him and the base toward which he is advancing. After forcing the runner back toward the base he has left you throw the ball to the protector of that base, then return to your position. Each base should be protected on run-up plays. Always be sure that you are one base ahead of the leading base runner so that you can protect that base if a runner tries to reach it.

Holding a base runner on first is very important. A steal puts a man in scoring position and a single will score him. Stand with your back foot on the pitching rubber with the front spike just over the edge of the rubber. All your weight should be on your back foot and your front foot far enough in front of the rubber to allow yourself perfect balance so that your front foot points a little toward first base. After you receive the catcher's sign, rest your elbows on your hips and hold your hands belt-high and directly in front of your body, the ball well hidden in your glove. This stance enables you to keep the runner close to the bag and enables you to make a quick throw to first. Never allow a base runner too big a lead off first, and don't waste time in your motion, pitching toward the batter.

In attempting to pick a base runner off first, you should make a throw that the first baseman can catch about knee-high and on the side of the base (second base) the runner is trying to reach. This gives the first baseman a good chance to tag out the runner trying to slide back into the base.

Your stance should be practically the same when there is a base runner leading off second. If you see a chance to pick that runner off, you should make a quick sidearm or three-quarter overhand throw. It is no longer a hard and fast rule that a right-handed pitcher should turn his body toward first base or that a left-hander should turn toward third base when such a pick-off attempt is made.

Use the motion that comes easiest to you.

Never waste time on the runner at first base when base runners are on first and second. Always watch the runner nearest home plate. It is important that you vary the "looks" you give those runners, for if you get into the habit of always looking at them just once or always twice they will know when to get the running start on you.

Pitchers need to acquire many skills, but there is one very few ever achieve: the ability to hit. They are considered an automatic out the moment they leave the on-deck circle, and one who can lay down that all-important bunt or chip in with a single is a great asset to his team. Many a pitcher who has been hurling a fine ball game has had to give in to a pinch-hitter in the late innings when his team needs a run to tie the game or go ahead. Pitchers should be good bunters, able to sacrifice a runner into scoring position. They should see that they get their share of batting practice, for being the ninth good hitter in the batting order will add more than a few years to their baseball careers. Pick up a bat at every opportunity and work out with the batting-practice pitchers. There is hardly a pictcher anywhere in baseball who would rather get a base hit than a strikeout against the heaviest slugger in the league.

There are many ways you can help yourself win ball games. When you are watching the game from the dugout, carefully study all opposing batters to detect any weaknesses they might have. Take mental notes of other pitchers, particularly the big winners, and see what they do when facing certain situations, or what they do not do. As a pitcher, you should never stop learning. Those who felt they knew it all made little or no impression on the record books.

Lose no time getting to the shower after the strain of hurling nine innings, for muscles can quickly stiffen if not allowed to cool off properly. Chronic sore arms have spelled the doom of many promising pitchers.

CHAPTER FOUR

BACK OF THE PLATE

The catcher, also called the backstop, is second in importance only to the manager of a ball club when it comes to directing the play. His defensive armor, mask, chest protecter, and shin guards, are called the "tools of ignorance" by his teammates, for the catcher absorbs more physical punishment than any other player on the field. Foul tips rattle off every part of his body, and at times he gets nicked by the swing of a bat.

Contrary to the general belief that all catchers must possess a powerful physique, they come in various sizes, but it must be admitted that a tall catcher has an advantage over shorter backstops when he has to haul down a high pitch or a reach for a pitch wide of the plate. To be a good catcher you require strong hands and a powerful throwing arm, and you must be able to throw quickly and accurately.

As the catcher, you are in charge of the other players when your team is on the field defensively, and you should study every opposing batter for his weaknesses and his habits. You must know the right pitch to call in all kinds of situations, and you are responsible for maintaining the morale of the other eight players on your team.

The best position for your feet back of the plate is to have your left foot out in front of your right foot by no more than three inches. Your knees should be spread apart. This catching position keeps you well balanced and puts you in good throwing position. For signalling, your left arm rests on your left leg and your right arm on your upper thigh. You are in a crouch when you give the sign to the pitcher, your body still well balanced. Just before the ball is delivered you rise up on the balls of your feet, giving the pitcher the "target angle." If men are on base, you catch the ball as quickly as possible and assume the correct throwing position to stop a runner from stealing a base.

Signals or signs delivered to the pitcher by the catcher must be from a squatting position and by means of the fingers. They must be well hidden from opposing players or coaches. The catcher's knees should be close enough together and at an angle that will make it impossible for the other team's coaches at first and third base to make out the signs. The signalling hand is covered by the mitt by laying the mitt over the left leg near the knee. One finger showing could mean a curve or a fast ball, two fingers a half-speed pitch, and

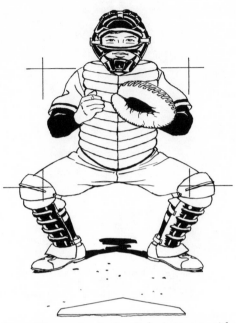

The Strike Zone. The catcher is the pitcher's target, with a four-corner boundary marked by the right and left shoulders and the right and left knees. In the catching position, the catcher's legs are spread wide apart, left foot slightly ahead of right. He should stay comfortably balanced on the balls of his feet, ready to shift in any direction.

three fingers the slow ball, and so on. A catcher must mix up his signals, never using the same sequence for a succeeding batsman.

Catch as close to the batsman as possible, without interfering with his swing. The average backstop stands so close that a bat just misses the tip of his mitt by not more than an inch. To avoid finger injuries, keep your bare hand in a half-closed, relaxed position. All catchers try to influence an

In the signalling position, the catcher should be balanced on the balls of his feet and have his legs spread apart. The right wrist and hand are on the upper thigh of the right leg.

umpire's call and get that called strike if they can, so catch a high ball *down* and a low ball *up*. The difference between an ordinary catcher and a star backstop is his ability to catch low balls and balls hit into the dirt in front of the plate.

Practice catching low-thrown balls as often as you can, for you will have to handle many of those pitches during the course of a ball game. You must have the ability to shift rapidly and this takes constant practice. Assume the catcher's position and move the left foot to the right and step to the side with the right foot. Practice shifting to the right, to the left, forward, and sideways, always switching the foot you use first in the direction in which you are going. You can practice shifting in a gym or in your room.

Your throw to the second baseman when a base runner tries to steal from first is possibly one of the most important defensive plays you will have to make. When you make that throw, your balance should rest on the back foot, whether it be the left or the right, the other foot acting as a guide. It is best to develop the habit of throwing off the right foot. Your first consideration when a base runner is trying to steal is to get the ball away as fast as you can. At the second you receive the ball, take it out of your glove without a single movement of the glove and bring it in a direct line to the throwing position. Accuracy, do not forget, counts as much as the speed you put behind the throw. The catcher's throwing arm should never drop below the waist when he assumes the throwing position.

You should never throw the ball as hard as you're able to any base. It should be a snap throw, a "peg," the ball raised back as far as the ear before it is let go. Constant practice on getting the ball away is advisable, and you will soon learn the sufficient amount of speed you need in getting that ball to a baseman so that he may handle it easily. Accuracy comes first.

When you have a base runner on first, you

must be alert and keep your body in throwing position with every pitch. Never try to throw out a runner leading off second base unless you catch that player napping, his mind anywhere but on the ball game. Wild throws to second lead to runs on the part of the other team. A catcher seldom tries to pick a runner off third. If you make such an attempt, be sure to throw the ball on the *inside* of the third base bag, for a throw to the outside of the base cannot be handled by your third baseman.

In a bases loaded situation you have to look for the double play in the event a ball is hit to the infield, and you should step out in front of the plate, keeping your pivot foot in contact with the front of the plate. If the ball is hit to the shortstop (6) he throws to you (2) to force the runner coming in from third at the plate and then you fire to the first baseman (3) to complete the double play.

When a base runner is trying to score from second on a base hit to the outfield, brace yourself for the play at the plate and always keep in mind that the best catchers play the man and the ball instead of the ball and the man. Never try to tag a runner before the ball is firmly held in your mitt. And brace yourself hard because a runner will try and knock you loose from that ball.

Never leave your position back of the plate to back up throws when a base runner is in scoring position, at second or third. Otherwise you should

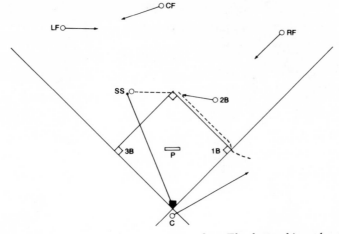

There is one out and a base runner on first. The batter hits a hard grounder to short, forcing the lead runner at second. The second baseman, trying for the double play, throws wild to first, the runner moving to second when the catcher fails to back up the throw to first. Fielders are in position to back up throws to second if the catcher had been alert in playing his position.

back up throws from second to first and all throws from the first baseman to the pitcher when the pitcher has to leave the mound to cover first base. You back up first base on *all* attempts at double plays.

Catching high foul balls within range of the plate calls for sharp reflexes and quick movements on your part. Make allowances for any wind that may be blowing and get directly under the ball so that either a sliding step forward or backward will allow you to make the catch. Let your infielders catch the fly balls hit over the infield when it is possible for them to do so. And shout any infielder off who happens to come into your territory for a

When you are blocking the plate for the tag, brace yourself and make sure that the ball is held firmly in your mitt.

fly ball to avoid a collision with that player.

When a ball is fouled high over the plate or in your territory, slide your mask up quickly and toss it away in the direction opposite to the ball to avoid tripping over it. Never make a basket-catch of a high foul ball, close to your waist. The mitt should be held a little over your head, the wrist bent back to allow the ball to drop into the pocket. As soon as the ball settles into the mitt, the other hand should immediately trap it there. If a ball delivered to a right-handed hitter comes over the inside corner of the plate and the sound of the bat indicates a foul pop-up, you should spin around to the

To field a pop foul, the catcher slides his mask back and locates the ball. Then he slides his mask up and flips it away in the direction opposite to that of the incoming foul ball. He holds the mitt a little above his head, with wrists bent back to let the ball drop into the pocket.

left, for the ball will go that way. If a pitch over the outside of the plate is fouled, you should whirl to the right. It is not possible for an outside pitch to be fouled over a catcher's left shoulder or an inside pitch to be fouled over his right shoulder.

As stated before, the catcher directs the defensive team, so you must be in a position to field many bunts. Always move forward from your normal catching stance when a batter "shortens up" on his bat and use both your glove and your bare hand when scooping up a rolling, twisting bunted ball. One-handed pickups are not for a catcher still learning his trade.

Try to avoid the three errors that many catchers commit:

1. Reaching down with your hands for a low pitch. Crowd such a pitch into the dirt and block it with your body to keep it from rolling back to the stands or glancing off your glove far enough on either side of the plate to allow a base runner to score or to advance a base.

2. Moving around behind the plate when the pitcher is already starting his motion. Make yourself a stationary target or the pitcher's control will suffer.

3. Neglecting to hold hands in the same position before each pitch. Continually holding the glove up for a fast ball and dropping it down to signal for a curve ball tips off the opposing batsmen and their coaches as to what kind of pitch to expect.

You, as the catcher, "handle" the pitchers. You should know the strength and weakness of the pitchers as well as those of your opponents. You are a better judge than your manager a great deal of the time when a decision to change pitchers is made, for you should know if the pitcher has lost the zing on his fast ball or if his curves are not breaking, or if too many pitches are missing the strike zone. A trip to the mound, a few words of encouragement at the right time, goes a long way to keep a pitcher from an early shower. As often as it is practical, you would do well to call for the pitch your battery mate has the most confidence in when he is behind the batter in the ball-and-strike count.

When you know which pitcher is selected to start a ball game, it is a good idea to be his warm-up catcher for a few minutes, for it will give you an opportunity to see if he's really ready. If his speed is off, if he is pressing, and his control is not what it should be, you should inform the manager that a change in the pitching assignment be made. Know your pitcher. Know what he can do and see that he does it. Your job is to catch a winning game! Remember, as the catcher for your team, the game is always in front of you. You are the director. Only you and the batsman are in front of the pitcher and only through your actions will the pitcher be aware of the feelings and movements of the players behind him. It is your responsibility to see that the outfielders are in their proper positions according to the type of hitter at the plate and to remind your teammates by a show of fingers the number of outs that have been made. The importance of your moral support to the other eight players on the team cannot be over emphasised.

CHAPTER FIVE

PLAYING FIRST BASE

There are some things that you will only learn from long experience. The next time you're in a big league ball park or viewing a game on television, watch the veteran first baseman "feel" or kick at the bag just before he takes his position. It is not due to nervousness on his part; he is mentally measuring the location of the bag while his eyes are elsewhere. Watch his feet carefully and profit by it. You will note how he shifts from right to left on the wild throws from the infielders, his right foot on the bag when bad throws are made in the direction of right field, and his left foot on the bag when erratic throws are made on the coaching box side. He never gets caught with his legs crossed.

There are times when the pitcher concentrates so much on a dangerous hitter that he forgets there is a base runner leading off first and makes no attempt to pick him off. It is the first baseman's duty to ask the umpire for time and walk to the mound to remind the pitcher that the other team has the *steal* sign on.

When there is a base runner on first and a ground ball is hit to you at first base, you start the 3-7-3 double play if you throw to the shortstop covering second. After fielding the ball and throwing to second, you immediately go back to your base to take the throw back from the shortstop. Many times a first baseman will make the first part of the play and then find himself in an awkward position because he did not glance at the bag before taking the return throw. If his foot is off the bag, he misses the double play.

Lazy "Let George Do It" first basemen do not last long in real competition. They are the players that hang back and let the catcher field the pop-ups they could easily have handled themselves. Unless you are willing to give one hundred per cent every minute of a ball game, you should not even think about wanting to be a big leaguer. The desire you absolutely must have is not there.

Many baseball fans are mistaken in their belief that first base is the easiest position to play on a ball field. Possibly they came to this conclusion during the past few years when big league managers shifted aging outfielders, whose bats were still hot, to first base to save wear and tear on their legs. To be a good first baseman you must be tall or at least of medium height, have a good reach, and possess the ability to make pickups of low throws from the infielders.

The first baseman takes his position in the infield in such a spot that demands no extra effort on his part to reach the bag in time to get set for the throw. His playing depth varies. If the batsman is a slow runner, he can play deeper than usual, if a fast runner is at bat, he must play closer to the base. There is no set rule as to how far he plays off the bag. When not playing close to the bag to hold a runner on, station yourself just far enough away from the base to allow you to get back and take a throw from an infielder without extra effort. When holding a runner on first, you should keep your pivot foot, the left, near the front edge of the bag and your front, right foot, facing the pitcher. When the attempted pick-off play is made by the pitcher, you should catch it knee-high if possible and put the ball on the runner with a sweeping motion.

There is one exception to the rule covering a first baseman's position off first. That is when a sure left-field hitter is up at the plate. In this case it is advisable for you to hold the runner as close to the bag as possible and to stand a few feet behind the base line, not on the bag but in a direct line with your regular position. This position will enable you to field a hard-hit ground ball pulled your way and to hold the runner on at the same time. If the batsman is a sure right-handed hitter, you stand in your regular position behind the base line.

As soon as the ball is hit to any infielder, break immediately for the bag, and take a position in front of it with your feet stationary, astride the bag.

When holding a man on first, the first baseman should keep his pivot foot near the front edge of the bag.

Before the throw reaches you, be ready to shift instantly to the right or left if the ball is thrown wide.

When the other team's strategy calls for a batter to bunt, you should not waste time rushing toward the plate as the batter "shortens up" on the bat. You should be alert to your catcher's instructions as to where you should throw the ball. He will tell you to either throw to second for a force play or to your second baseman covering first. If the ball is bunted toward third, hustle back to first base to make a possible putout there.

There is always the possibility of a batsman who has made a base hit to the outfield to try and stretch the hit into an extra base, then suddenly change his mind and head back to first. Be ready to take the throw from the outfielder and join in the run-up play when the runner is caught between first and second. If a base runner is caught off first by your pitcher's pick-off throw and breaks for second, throw the ball to the shortstop covering that bag, then retreat to first base to make the putout in the event of a run-up play.

A first baseman handles ground balls in the manner of all the other infielders. Play the ball in front of you as much as possible. With your hands in this position, you have the opportunity to pick up the ball in front of you in case of a fumble, whereas if your hands are even with your feet, the chances are the ball will bounce behind you. Your glove or mitt should be kept as close to the ground as possible especially when fielding grounders that hug the dirt. If a ball takes a bad bounce and your hands cannot be brought up quickly enough, you have a chance to block it with your body.

Your eyes should follow the ball until it settles in your glove. Do not lift your head, for if your eyes fail to see a ball bounce, it could get past you for an error. Never cross your feet or legs fielding a ground ball. Your feet should be apart in as near the correct throwing position possible in order that you can throw to a baseman covering your base without loss of time.

With a runner in scoring position at second base, you play your position on base hits to the outfield, but on all fly balls to the outfield that have to be fielded to stop a base runner from advancing, you must back up that base to which the throw is made.

Perhaps the hardest play you will have to make

Fred Ferreira demonstrates the correct position for fielding grounders. Put your glove close to the ground in front of you, ready to scoop up the ball, keeping your other hand ready to take the ball out for the quick throw. You should be in a crouching position, back bent, with your eyes on the ball.

Larry Brown helps a young player perfect his fielding position.

as a first baseman is when a throw comes to you on the left side of the bag directly into the path of the base runner coming from the plate. Catch the ball with your gloved hand and in almost the same motion jump away from the base line the instant you catch the ball. If there is time enough, it would be wise to step all the way off the bag and tag the runner with both hands.

Avoid going too far into the second baseman's territory to field a ground ball. Hours of practice will teach you how far you can go out of your territory.

Both right-handed and left-handed first basemen should stretch out as far as possible to meet a ball thrown by an infielder. The extra second or two you will save often means the difference between an out and a man on base. Make that stretch whether it is a good throw or one you have to

Perfecting the stretch at base may often mean the difference between an out and a man on base. If the throw comes to the right, the baseman touches the bag with the toe of his left foot.

scoop up from the dirt. The first baseman has to handle more bad throws than any other infielder and most of these should be caught with the gloved hand alone.

There are times when an infield is drawn in to keep a base runner from scoring from third. If a ground ball is hit to you in that situation, you should run in toward the plate after fielding it and throw the ball to the catcher in view of a possible run-up play on the man trying to score. Remember, that as the first baseman you are expected to be a good back-up man and catch or cut off all wild throws to the position you have taken and complete any play that presents itself.

When drawn off the bag to field a ground ball, never toss or lob the ball to the pitcher covering your base. Your throw should be letter high and with some steam behind it, and if you think you can beat the base runner to the bag yourself after fielding the ball, yell at or wave the pitcher off. Failure to do this could cause serious injury to one or both players.

In some cases you will find that you have to throw the ball to second base without hitting a base runner, so take precautions in aiming your throw. If throwing from the infield, aim the ball at the shortstop who should be stationed to the left side of second base. If throwing from your position at first base, be sure to aim it at the short-stop playing to the right of second base.

You are the cutoff man when certain situations arise. (Cutting off means intercepting a ball thrown from the outfield when you see no chance of the throw putting out a man at the plate and throwing to a base a runner is trying to reach). With a runner trying to score from second, you line yourself up with the throw from the outfield 50 to 60 feet from home plate and if you see that you cannot prevent the runner from scoring, cut off the throw and either hold the hit to a single or try to cut down the runner trying to reach second. You are the relay man on extra base hits inside the right field foul line who takes the throw from deep in the out-field and then throws to the plate to cut off a run.

Very few outfielders can throw all the way to the plate from deep outfield positions, and the relay man, always an infielder, makes the catch and then throws into the plate. First basemen back up all throws from center field, right field, and second base.

On all throws that are not wide of the bag, the left-handed first baseman keeps his left foot on the bag and extends his right foot; the right-hand man keeps his right foot on the bag and extends his left foot. On any ball thrown to first by the catcher, the first baseman should take the throw inside the diamond lest the ball hit the runner. This does not apply to a pick-off play but when the catcher has to throw to first after fielding a bunt or after a dropped third strike by the catcher.

CHAPTER SIX

PLAYING SECOND BASE

Second base is often called the keystone sack because more crucial plays, involving the second baseman and shortstop, take place at that part of the diamond. A runner standing on that base is said to be at the "pick up" station, for he will generally score on a single.

The ability to field ground balls is the first requirement of any infielder. To play second base you must have "loose" wrists, be quick on your feet, and be able to make fast and accurate throws even though you have no time in which to set yourself. In fielding ground balls or catching low throws you have to play the ball directly in front of you, and as the ball hits your hands, quickly draw them in toward your body to guard against a rebound. Keeping the ball in front of you enables you to recover a fumble and still throw your man out at first. You should be able to throw sidearm, underhand, or overhand. Always be ready for that bad hop!

Always be careful not to cross your feet or legs in fielding a ground ball. The feet should be apart in as near a correct throwing position as possible so that you can save time in starting the throw to a baseman. Playing a ground ball with the feet close together makes you take an unnecessary step before you throw.

When a base runner is running toward second to steal that base, the base bag should be between your feet as you take the throw from the catcher. When you catch the ball, hold it in the glove placed on the side of the base into which the runner has to slide.

If there are two players on a ball club that have to work as a team, it is the second baseman and shortstop. They guard that vital spot in the diamond known as "up the middle" where many a ball game has been won or lost. As the second baseman you must have the utmost confidence in the shortstop's ability and know his style of play as well as your own.

Play to the strength of the batters. Do they usually hit to the right or the left side of the dia-mond? Or up the middle? Watch the catcher's every sign to the pitcher and shift your position accordingly. Most right-handed batsmen hit the ball to center field or left center and left-handed batsmen hit to right or right center. Form the habit of making a move toward second base after every pitch that passes by the batter when there is a runner on first. This will stop an attempt on the part of a base runner on first to make a delayed steal.

Hardly a game goes by when a fly ball is not hit back of second base beyond the reach of the outfielders. Sometimes it is within the shortstop's range. If you, as the second baseman, hear him yell, "I've got it!," lose no time getting back to your position. If the catch is not made, you can prevent the batter from reaching second.

Field any ball hit into your territory. If one gets by you, do not lose any time getting back to your position to help out in any play that may follow, like backing up the first baseman or taking a relay throw from an outfielder.

Double plays for the most part are started by the second baseman or shortstop. When the shortstop fields a ground ball, you come over fast from your position in a direct line with the throw coming from the shortstop. Be sure to hit the bag with your pivot foot. Your other foot should hit the ground as nearly a direct line as possible between first and home plate. To bring yourself clear of the onrushing base runner and complete the double play, it is best to throw to the first baseman sidearm, bringing your arm across the front of your body. At times, however, a base runner will try to take the second baseman out of the play with a hard slide before the baseman can make the throw to first. In the opinion of many fans this maneuver, al-

72

As soon as the ball is caught and held firmly, the infielder locates the target, puts his weight on his rear foot, and throws the ball in one smooth motion.

though legal, should be confined to the gridiron.

Two difficult plays for you to make as the second baseman are:

1. When a slow ball is hit toward your position. You cannot afford to wait for it to come to

To start the double play, the infielder should throw sidearm to the first baseman without taking a single step.

you. Charge it and field it on the run, then throw quickly to first with a quick underhand motion. More often than not you will have to scoop up this kind of hit with your bare hand and only constant practice will make you adept at this difficult play.

2. When a ball is hit to your right near second base. (Considered the hardest play a second baseman is called upon to make) You have to go after the ball at full speed and throw all your weight on your right foot as you glove the ball. Then you come up short, maintaining sufficient balance to make the sidearm throw across your body to the first baseman.

A state of confusion often exists between you and the shortstop when a steal of second is threatened by a base runner on first, so a signal between you and the shortstop, one to the other, should be given depending upon the type of pitch that is going to be thrown to the batter.

Never venture too far into the outfield to take a relay throw from an outfielder. Bear in mind that you are responsible for the short and accurate throw to the plate to cut off a possible run. And after catching the ball from the outfielder, always be alert for instructions from the shortstop as to whether you should make the play at home plate or try to cut down a base runner trying to advance.

When the other team has a runner on first base and none out, you must expect the batter at the plate to bunt. Play your regular position and keep your eye on the batter. The first baseman is ready to charge into the infield to field the bunt. The catcher, anticipating the bunt, calls for a pitch wide of the plate, a waste ball. The moment that first baseman leaves the bag you move quickly over to cover it. You will reach the bag in time to take the throw from the catcher in the event he has fielded a bunt in front of the plate. As soon as you make the putout, rush toward third base to be in a position to stop the man who has been sacrificed to second from going to third.

As a second baseman you protect your base on all hits to left field. You go out toward the outfielder on all hits to right field but return to the infield if the ball is properly fielded to back up the shortstop for any play attempted at second base.

The baseman should keep the ball high when he runs down the base runner.

When the opposing team has a runner on first and a steal of second is expected, you should know whether or not your pitcher is going to throw a fast ball or a curve. Having less speed than a fast ball, the curve is most always hit into left field.

76

You should always let your pitcher know when you are going to protect the bag for an attempted steal so that he may throw pitches that the batsman cannot hit into right field, through the hole you have to vacate in order to cover your base.

When a runner is caught off second and you are holding the ball, run the base runner toward third. The shortstop covers the base you have left unprotected.

Always avoid the mistake of underhanding any ball hit to you near second base for a putout at that bag. Those throws often go wild. Snap the ball from your correct fielding position with a back-hand motion. On all hits to left field stay on the bag, but always go out on the outfield grass on hits to right field. If the outfielder throws to second base, it is your duty to back up the shortstop taking the throw.

There are several defensive situations which call for a shift in the location of infielders. As the second baseman do you play deep, shallow, or very close in? The last position is always set up when a base runner is on third waiting to score on a grounder to the infield. Playing close in, on the grass, gives you a head start on any ball hit your way and enables you to make a hard, quick throw to the plate.

CHAPTER SEVEN

THE SHORTSTOP'S GAME

The belief that the shortstop has the most difficult position on a ball club is debatable, but if you choose to play that position on the team you will be a very busy man. There have been middle-sized shortstops in the major leagues but the tall man, everything considered, has a distinct advantage at that place in the infield. To be a good shortstop you must have wrists that are loose and flexible. Rigid wrists and forearms lead to errors. Like all infielders you must be schooled in the proper use of the glove and hands; the face of the glove and the palm of the other hand have to face the ball as it comes to you whether off the hitter's bat or a throw to you from another player.

As the shortstop, you protect second base on all hits to right field or when the ball is bunted in front of the plate. In an assist, to start a double play, get rid of the ball from the position in which you field it, and throw to the second baseman shoulder-high. If you are some distance away from second base when you field the ball, be sure to throw it with plenty of power behind it.

On double plays you will often find yourself the pivot man at second base. With a runner on first only and a ball hit to the second baseman, go to the keystone sack on the run, hit the bag with your pivot foot, and throw the ball to first base for the attempt to complete the double play. If, with a runner on first, the first baseman starts the double play after fielding a ground ball, and throws to you after touching his own base, make certain that you tag the runner out at second base. This would not be a force play.

You will be faced with three difficult plays as a shortstop: Fielding a batted ball that bounces high over the pitcher's head, fielding a fly ball hit to shallow left field or center field; and fielding a ball hit to the left of the third baseman. In the first instance you must field the ball on the dead run, whirl, and throw to first base. You will not have time to set yourself for the throw, and only long hours of practice will enable you to make this play with the required accuracy. As you field the ball, put most of your weight on your right foot in braking to a stop, and at almost the same instant balance yourself for the throw to first base, which should be overhand with all your power behind it. On this kind of play every second counts.

Be a heads-up shortstop. Give some kind of signal to your outfielders as to the type of pitch

The shortstop often becomes the pivot man at second base on double plays. He tags the bag with his right toe, steps over the bag, and throws to first base.

the pitcher is going to throw to the batsman, for it gives the outfielders a running start on balls hit beyond the infield.

Have a signal arrangement with your pitcher for trapping runners off second base. Always cover that base when there is a runner on first and a sure right-field hitter is at bat. One situation that calls for the hit and run on the part of the opponents is when they have a left-handed hitter up at the plate. Hit and run means that the runner is off with the pitch, and the batter must try to hit safely behind him. The batter will try to hit through the "hole" at short, so never leave your shortstop position too quickly in order to cover second base on an attempted steal by the runner on first. You can protect yourself on this play by moving a step or two nearer second base just before the pitcher has assumed his correct pitching position. This movement on your part, however, should not be too apparent to your opponents.

As the shortstop you will be responsible for fielding fly balls, fair or foul, in back of the third baseman, that the left fielder does not call for. You take all throws to second base when balls are hit back to the pitcher, when the play has to be made to that bag. There is an exception: When you're playing to the extreme right of your normal position to protect against a right-handed pull hitter, one that invariably hits pitches into left field. Then you let the second baseman take the throw. Before this play comes up, you should make the pitcher aware of the situation.

Every strategic move you make as the shortstop should be without a moment of indecision, and these certain plays should become routine after constant practice:

1. Back up the second baseman when he has to come to the bag to take a throw from an out-

The fielder should take a comfortable but alert stance and be ready to shift to any direction as the ball comes his way.

fielder, when there is a runner on first.

2. Go out into left field for a possible relay whenever a ball is hit to that field. If the outfielder makes the catch or fields a base hit cleanly, go back to the bag and take the throw from the outfielder. If the ball has been hit deep, then you go out on the grass to take the relay.

3. When there is a runner on second and you're sure a fly ball will be caught in left field and there is no chance for a relay, go to third base and take the throw from the outfielder. The third baseman will be backing up the play.

4. If, with a runner on third, the catcher makes a throw to that base for an attempted putout, you protect that base in case it involves a run-up play on the part of the third baseman and the catcher.

5. If a ground ball is hit to the third baseman, with a runner on third, immediately cover that base for the possible run-up play. Always be alert for cutoff plays.

As the shortstop you cannot afford to let down or take your mind off the game for a moment, and you should plan in advance what to do with the ball hit to you in various situations. Study the batters carefully and keep track of the number of outs that have been made, and keep in mind the speed of the runners that happen to be on the bases. Whether you're like a tall Marty Marion or a diminutive Phil Rizzuto does not matter. If you have the talent, you have every chance of becoming a good shortstop.

The position of play for a shortstop varies, according to the numbers of runners on base. With a runner on first, none out, and a bunt expected, you move in a step or two in line with home plate, ready to go to second to make the force out if the play is made to that base.

With runners on first and second, none out, and the bunt sign on for the other team, you move directly back of the base runner leading off second without leaving a hole at your fielding position. Your objective is to keep this runner close to second in order that he does not take too big a lead toward third. There is always the chance of a force play at third due to a poor bunt on the part of the batsman.

As a shortstop you will be faced with a play you might only have to make once in the course of a season. It occurs when runners are on first and third and the sign for a double steal is given by the coaches. When this starts, run quickly from your position after the ball has passed by the batsman to a spot on the diamond about a step in front of second base and in a direct line with home plate. Watch first for the runner on third who might be attempting to score. If he breaks for the plate, cut off the catcher's throw to second and then fire it back to the plate. If the man on third does not break for the plate, stay at the position you have originally taken, then take the catcher's throw and pivot around to make the tag on the runner trying to steal from first to second.

Two things must be kept in mind when the double steal situation presents itself: What is the score? Is the game in the late innings? These factors should determine whether you should try for the runner at the plate, especially if he represents the winning or tying run. If your team has a safe lead and you are in the eighth or ninth inning, the steal of home does not matter too much. On such a play the chances of putting both men out stealing are slim indeed.

CHAPTER EIGHT

THE HOT CORNER

The third baseman, no matter what you might have heard, does not need a stronger throwing arm than any other infielder, for he is the closest defensive man to the batter at the plate which gives him that extra second or two to complete a play to the first baseman.

If you're well over medium height, can throw the ball from any position in which you field it, and are skilled in fielding swinging bunts, then you are qualified to play third base. Your normal position should be about ten feet behind the bag and about the same distance from the left field foul line. Play deep for slow runners and about on a line with third base for the fast runners. If you expect the batter to bunt, play well in on the grass, inside the diamond. Charge in toward the plate as soon as the batter shortens up to bunt.

It is said of the very best third basemen that "they either do or they don't" because of the many plays that require split-second decisions. The balls

This third baseman crouches in readiness as the runner comes in.

that drive your way are for the most part very hard hit, and you have to block many of them with your body to prevent them getting by you and into the outfield. Perhaps the hardest play a third baseman will be called upon to make is fielding the swinging bunt. As the ball trickles slowly toward you, rush in on it at full speed, scoop it up with your bare hand, and, off-balance, throw it underhand to the first baseman. If the ball rolls far enough toward you, however, you will have time to use your glove hand and can make the overhand throw to first.

If your pitcher, catcher, or first baseman fields a bunt, you should quickly return to your position in order to get set for a possible play on the base runner trying to reach third base after the putout at first is made.

The third baseman's normal depth, his correct position on the defense, is determined by the speed of the batter at the plate, the ball and strike count on the batter, the score, and the inning of the game. High school coaches recommend that third basemen play a couple of steps into the diamond and come in fast on all bunts and make the play to first or second according to instructions by the catcher. He should never throw on his own but must obey the catcher's call.

If you are a third baseman, you should always keep your eye on the batsman, not on the pitcher, while the ball is being pitched. You will be able to get a better jump on the ball, especially if the hitter lays down a bunt in your direction. When the ball is hit back to the pitcher, never fail to break toward the middle of the diamond to field balls deflected off the pitcher's glove.

There are certain basic plays a third baseman must keep in his mind. When there is a runner on first and a base hit goes to the outfield, stand at your position to take a throw from the outfielder. If the ball is hit into right field "behind the runner," you will have little chance of stopping a fast base runner from advancing to third; but after getting the throw from the right fielder you must try to cut down the batter trying to reach second on the base hit.

A third baseman may be involved in two kinds of double-play situations. First, a play that never fails to stir the fans, is the 5-4-3 double play called "around the horn," the ball traveling from the third baseman (5), to the second baseman (4), to the first baseman (3). This play can only take place when there is a runner on first, the other bases unoccupied. Secondly, with men on second and third and the ball hit toward you close to the bag, start the double play by stepping on third for the force on the lead runner. Then throw to the first baseman for the double play. On the scorecard you would mark down the play 5-3, only the third baseman and the first baseman being involved.

When there is a runner on third, protect that base on all ground balls hit your way and always stay at your station on all fly balls to the outfield, except when, with only one out, a runner on third tries to score on a long fly ball, a sacrifice fly to left field. Then you come in on the grass as the "stationary" man to handle a possible relay from the outfielder.

Another situation you will face as a third baseman calls for not the slightest hesitation on your part. With a base runner on third and a ground ball hit to you, make dead certain that the base runner is not going to try to score before you commit yourself and throw to first for the putout. If the runner does try to score, then throw to the catcher and protect the plate on the run-up play, the shortstop taking over your position at third.

It is your duty as a third baseman to field all

fair or foul pop-ups between your position and the catcher and outside the third base foul line. Often a mix-up occurs in such a situation, both the catcher and the third baseman going after the ball. Either one should shout the other off, yelling "I've got it," to avoid a collision and a dropped ball. Pop flies such as these should be caught on a level with your eyes, the palm of your glove up, the bare hand ready to trap the ball in the pocket of the glove. Balls that you have to catch close to the stands generally have to be made with one hand; otherwise, use both hands in making this kind of play.

When taking a throw to your base, always straddle the bag, and if a base runner is sliding in, place your gloved hand holding the ball in front of the bag so that the runner will slide right into it. A firm grip of the ball in the pocket of your glove must be kept, for there is always the possibility that an aggressive base runner will try to kick the ball loose from your glove.

Like all infielders a third baseman must study the batters, especially those who hit right-handed, for they naturally hit toward the left side of the diamond or up the middle. The fault you have to avoid is playing too close to the bag and being caught out of position, leaving a big hole for the hitter between third and short. When a skillful bunter is at bat, you should come up on the balls of your feet at every delivery made by the pitcher to give you that added start on a bunted ball.

Third basemen should spend time practicing fielding the swinging bunt.

During the course of a ball game you will find yourself playing the role of the cutoff man. In order to cut off all throws to the plate by an outfielder, you will have to be a cutoff man when there is a runner on second and a base hit goes into left field if there is no chance to put the runner out at the plate. An infielder is generally nearby instructing you to either let the throw go by or cut it off. The cutoff of a ball thrown by an outfielder to the infield at the proper time and executed perfectly is an all-important defensive move in preventing runners from getting into scoring position. The third baseman only acts as cutoff man on balls hit to left field.

There is one very difficult play you will have to make at the hot corner: when you have to field a bunted ball between the mound and the third base line. It is within the reach of both you and the pitcher. Suppose the base runner that was on second runs for third, and the bunter races toward first. Here again there is the danger of a mix-up between you and the pitcher but one can be avoided if, beforehand, you check with the pitcher in anticipation of just such a situation. The pitcher, in most cases, is moving toward third on the play and is in a better position to try and cut down the runner going into that base. You, the third baseman, will have your back to third base and your best move would be to try and get the putout at first. This is a real heads-up play and must be made without a moment of indecision.

There are five very important points for you, as a third baseman, to keep firmly in your mind:

1. Never leave a base uncovered.

2. On all fumbles by other infielders watch for runners over-running bases.

3. Know the strength and weaknesses of your teammates, how much ground they have the ability to cover, and be willing to cover more than your share of territory.

4. Never throw the ball if you see no chance of getting your man. Bluff the throw; you may get

The correct way for a third baseman to field a swinging bunt. He should scoop up the ball with his bare hand and throw underhand to the first baseman.

a putout on another player trying to advance a base on the expected throw.

5. When you catch a man off base, make sure you run him back to the base from which he came. No more than two throws should be necessary. Keep your arm cocked and bluff a throw once or twice. It often slows the runner up long enough for you to tag him out. Do not make a long throw to another teammate involved in the run-down, unless he keeps moving. Run toward him with the ball until he makes his move, then throw it.

CHAPTER NINE

INFIELD STRATEGY

A tight defense contributes as much to a winning ball club as do batsmen driving in runs. The main defensive requirement is keeping the opposing base runners from a scoring position, at second and third base. When should the infield be drawn in to prevent a run and when should it play in close to look for the double play even if it means giving up a run? To decide, even the smartest manager must take certain factors into consideration and be sure that the strategy will not backfire: the ability of his pitcher and that of the batsman, the speed of the base runners, and the possibility of an error. A drawn-in infield gives the offensive team the advantage. There is a saying around the big leagues that with an infield drawn in a .200 hitter adds 100 points to his batting average.

All players on a team should be aware of the infield fly rule. Most young players believe that a hitter of an infield fly is automatically out only when first or first and third base are occupied, but this is not the case. The rule (Rule 44, Section 8 of the Official Rules of Baseball) was made to stop a player from trapping a ball and making a double play. Specifically, the rule states that an infield fly which can be caught by an infielder with ordinary effort when first and second or first, second, and third are occupied before two are out, is declared an out by the umpire even if an infielder drops the ball. The rule was made for the benefit of the base runners. They can run at their own risk. Any bunt that is caught in the air by an infielder or catcher is not an infield fly.

Infielders should be aware of the catcher's signs to the pitcher. If a curve is correctly pitched to a left-handed batter, it can only be hit to right field. The second baseman, first baseman, and right fielder will be in position to field the ball.

Many a base hit has been made when the bases have been moved out of position. All infielders, before taking the defensive, should make sure to kick the bases back within the boundary lines of the diamond. Runners sliding into bases often kick them out of position. If any part of those bases happen to be outside the chalk or lime markings and are hit by a batted ball, the umpire has to declare it a base hit.

Infielders should handle the ball only when runners are trapped off the bases, and three men should be involved in the run-down. Make note of the following examples:

1. When a runner is caught off first base, the first baseman chases the runner toward second. The second baseman protects the first baseman's position, and the shortstop covers second. He catches the ball thrown to him by the first baseman, and turns the runner back toward first where the putout is made.

2. When a runner is caught off second base, the player making the throw chases the runner toward third and throws the ball to that base, the third baseman then turning the runner back toward second base where the putout is made. If the shortstop starts the play, he has to move quickly to cover third base.

3. When a runner is trapped off third base, that baseman chases the runner toward home plate, the shortstop covering third. The third baseman fires the ball into the catcher who in turn starts the runner back toward third and tags him out. Meanwhile, the third baseman is protecting the plate.

Infielders often find, after run-up plays are made, that two basemen are occupying the same base. The rules clearly state that two runners may not occupy the same base, but if, while the ball is alive (in play), two runners are touching a base, the following runner shall be out when he is tagged. The preceding runner is entitled to the base.

All infielders should watch the following play closely: when a runner is on first and a long fly ball is hit to the outfield, infielders should keep their eyes on the base runner if he rounds second base before the ball is caught. In his attempt to return to first he could fail to touch second base, and he could be called out. A base runner having to return to a base while the ball is still in play must touch all intervening bases. He will be called out if the throw-in from the outfield goes to any base he fails to touch or if he is tagged out with the ball in the hands of an infielder.

With the bases loaded and only one out, the defense should play deep, looking for the double play. If the ball is hit back to the pitcher or the third baseman, the twin killing must be to the catcher (2), to the first baseman (3), with one exception. If the batsman is an accurate left-field hitter, the first baseman plays in close; and if a ground ball is hit toward him, he throws to the catcher instead of second base. There are three defensive set-ups for infielders. A deep infield is the regular playing position. Moderately deep or halfway in means the infielders are stationed on, or about on, the imaginary base lines from first to second to third. Close-in puts them well in front of the imaginary base line. The close-in positions are always taken when there is a base runner on third threatening to score on an infield ground ball.

In the late innings, if your team is ahead by only one run and there is a runner on third with none out, the infield should play halfway, not too deep, depending upon the power of the hitter up at the plate. A fast runner on third could beat a throw to the plate if a ground ball were hit deep to the infield. Coming in on the ball gives the infielder that extra few seconds to get his throw into the catcher.

In the eighth or ninth inning, if the defensive team is leading by a single run, with one man out and a runner on third, the infield should play close-in to prevent the tying run from scoring and to keep the batsman from getting into scoring position.

There are occasions when a ball club, leading by one or two runs in the late innings of a game, finds itself backed against the wall. The bases are full and no one is out. The infield must play deep and look for the double play even at the cost of one run. If the ball is hit to the pitcher, third baseman, or first baseman, the double play must be made from catcher to first. If hit to the shortstop or second baseman, it is made from second to first.

Once again we must stress the importance of the cutoff, a ball thrown in from the outfield to an infielder. If executed properly it is one of the most crucial defensive plays in the game of baseball, for it prevents runners from advancing to scoring positions. In sandlot or high school ball, however, the outfielders do not have the strength in their arms to make the long throws, but infielders should try the cutoff if balls are hit shallowly to the outfield.

97

The first baseman is in the best position to be the cutoff man, as very few plays result at his position on balls hit beyond the infield. He does not have to guard his own base and can follow the ball thrown in by an outfielder and get in position to cut off the throw if he sees a runner trying for an extra base. One of the other infielders should yell, "Let it go!" or "Cut it off!" depending upon whether he thinks the first baseman has a play.

The shortstop is the cutoff man on all throws from right field or right center when he sees a possible play at third base and should station himself in a direct line between his base and the throw, approximately 60 feet from third base. In this case the third baseman will tell him to cut the ball off or let it go through. But if the shortstop is dead sure he can get a runner trying to advance a base, he should use his own judgement in making the play. The third baseman only cuts off throws on balls hit to left field when a runner is in scoring position.

CHAPTER TEN

PLAYING THE OUTFIELD

Center field is the key position in outfield play. The movements of the right and left fielders are governed by those made by the center fielder, and they should keep their same distance away from him at all times. If you are an outfielder, always watch your coaches, for they will regulate your playing depths according to the power of the hitter at the plate.

To play the outfield you must be a good judge of fly balls, be able to get a jump on ground balls hit your way, be fast of feet, and possess a strong overhand throwing arm. As the right fielder you are expected to make that long and accurate throw into the infield when a runner tries to advance from first to third on a base hit to right field. If you are the center fielder you should be the fastest man in the outfield, for you'll have more territory to cover. As the left fielder you require a strong throwing arm and must be adept at fielding ground balls. You are responsible for protecting the left field foul line on balls hit over or just inside the bag at third.

As the right fielder it is your duty to back up first base on all bunted balls and all plays made by the catcher to first base so that you will be in a position to field the ball in your territory in the event of an error or a wild throw. On all balls thrown from the third baseman or shortstop in the infield you should back up second base. The center fielder backs up second base when throws are made to that bag by the catcher or pitcher.

If you're playing left field, you back up all throws made to the left side of the diamond, and you back up third base when a runner, after a two base hit to right field, attempts to turn the hit into a triple, a three base hit. You also back up third base when a runner on second tries to get to third after a fly ball is caught and thrown into the infield by the right fielder.

The three outfielders, when a straightaway hitter is at bat, always divide the outfield area equally between them, the right fielder and left fielder playing well off the foul lines. Left-handed hitters have a tendency to pull the ball to the right side of the playing field, and right-handers hit to the opposite side of the field, so shift accordingly.

Before and during a ball game all outfielders should check the direction of any wind blowing over the ball park. If it is blowing in toward the infield, play in closer; and if toward the outfield, you should move back closer to the fences. Make allowances for crosswinds that can play tricks with fly balls or balls thrown into the infield.

In making a catch of a long fly ball hit your way, get a fast start on it and try to be in a position to throw it when you catch it; and if there is a runner or runners on the bases, you should have the base in mind to throw to before releasing the ball. Every throw an outfielder makes is overhand and it should reach the baseman on one hop. Throws on a direct line often go wide of the base or over a baseman's head. Never hold the ball for even the fraction of a second because base runners are always looking for that chance to make an extra base.

When catching a fly ball, extend your arms upward with the back of the glove and the back of the bare hand toward your face. "Basket" catches, when the glove and bare hand is held close to your chest or midriff, palms up, are for the likes of the great Willie Mays and not recommended for young ball players or for the average big league ball player. There are situations, of course, where you have to make a running one-handed catch, but whenever possible, use *both* hands.

Correctly judging a fly ball to the outfield takes hours and hours of practice. When it is over your head, never run backwards, but turn your body toward the ball and run, and at the right moment swing your body around to face the ball and make the catch. Often you will have to catch it

The outfielder catches the fly ball at his chest or higher. He uses both hands, his gloved hand to catch the ball and his bare hand to quickly cover the ball and if necessary take it out for the quick throw to the infield.

over your shoulder, but this play will also become routine if you work at it long enough. If you do, you will discover that you can give chase to a fly ball without having to look over your shoulder to see where it is. Seasoned outfielders can judge how far a ball to the outfield is hit by the sound of the bat, an instinct that comes only from years of play.

Certain fielding plays on the part of all outfielders are often influenced by the number of runs

102

their team is ahead or behind, the number of outs, and the number of innings already played. Putouts at the plate by outfielders are few and far between, and it is to your team's advantage at times to forget an attempt to throw the ball to a base to keep another runner from getting into scoring position.

As an outfielder you should always remember

Be sure to follow through on your throws.

that the first throw of a relay has to be a long and accurate one. The second throw made by the infielder if the play is going to home plate is the short one.

Fly balls within the reach of both you and an infielder should be fielded by you if possible, and always call out to the infielder, "I've got it!" to avoid a collision.

Coaches do not look with favor upon an outfielder trying the "shoe-string" catch, fielding the ball at the insteps before it hits the ground. If such a ball gets by you, it more often than not turns a single into a double or a triple. It is wiser to play it safe, fielding the ball on the bounce and allowing the one-base hit.

Use your arm sparingly in practice; it is your strongest defensive weapon, the reason for being at the outfield position you play. During practice experienced coaches should station a relay player halfway between the outfielders position and the player batting the practice fly balls to save wear and tear on the outfielders' arms on the throw-ins.

If you really desire to become a star outfielder, you would do well to pattern yourself after the Cincinnati Red's right fielder, Pete Rose, the man they call "Johnny Hustle." Watch Rose run in and off the field between innings. He even runs to first when given a base on balls. That is why you always find him in the National League lineup when the All-Star games come around. Never get the idea

For an incoming fly ball, you may need to hold up your glove to block out the sun.

that playing the outfield is a cinch. More demands are made on a flychaser's physical endurance than on any other player on the team, with the possible exception of the catcher.

When you have mastered the fundamentals of playing the outfield, you must learn to think along with the opposing hitters and get the jump on all balls hit to your territory. If you can acquire that knack, you will learn to be an outstanding outfielder.

CHAPTER ELEVEN

SWINGING THE BAT

Every ball player, whether he be a boy playing on a sandlot or a big leaguer in the Astrodome or Shea Stadium, eagerly awaits his turn at bat. Even most pitchers, notoriously weak hitters, like to take their swings at the ball, and the goal of all good batsmen is to hit as close to .300 as possible. A player's batting average is determined by dividing the number of hits he has made by his number of times at bat.

The fault of many hitters is their desire to hit the ball out of the park rather than use a natural easy swing and meet the pitched ball squarely. The good hitter hits the ball where it is pitched, and follows through with his body. Every ball player has his own batting style. No coach should try to change it unless a batter goes into a prolonged slump and has picked up some bad batting habits, like pulling away from the plate, using too low a crouch, dropping one shoulder as he swings, or standing to the extreme rear of the batter's box.

Remember these five essentials if you wish to become a reliable batsman:

1. Stance This is the foundation of your hitting. Stance includes how you set your feet in the batter's box, how you hold the bat, keep yourself in position for free body movement, and the correct balance.

2. Stride This is the step you take to put yourself in position to meet and hit the ball.

3. Control of the Plate If your bat can reach any pitch thrown in the strike zone—the width of the plate and from your armpits to your knees—you have the plate covered.

4. Hand Action Power is not only obtained by the hands, but also by the wrists and forearms. Many hitters put too much of their shoulders behind their swing.

5. Stroke The swing of the bat. Hit *up* on the low strike ball, swing *down* on the high pitched ball, and swing *through* on balls pitched right down the middle of the plate. Swinging through means that you should maintain a level swing.

Keep your head steady at all times, and never take your eyes off the pitcher from the time he delivers the ball until it comes across the plate. Stand closer to the rear of the batter's box than in front of it, with most of your weight on your rear foot, and keep your feet as close together as the position you have chosen will allow. Feet wide apart is the open stance, and feet closer together the closed stance.

Your step forward is the stride you take to

A good batting stance. Grip the bat firmly, with hands close together. Keep your feet comfortably apart and your body well balanced, left foot slightly ahead of right. Your knees should be slightly bent. Stand erect but not stiff, and keep your eyes on the pitcher.

put yourself in a position to hit the ball. You should stride the same distance regardless of the type of ball pitched. That step you take is straight toward the pitcher, and should not be more than 18 inches. It shifts the weight from the back foot to the front foot without affecting your balance. Never try to hit the ball before or after that stride is taken but at the very moment the weight of your body is on both feet. If you make contact with the ball at that instant, you have obtained perfect timing.

To be a consistently good batsman you must have excellent eyesight, a position at the plate in which you are most comfortable, and a good level swing. If you continue to have a very poor batting average for too long a time, your fault is most likely a loss of correct timing, bringing your bat around too quickly or too slowly. Many managers and coaches have tried countless remedies, and one that seems to bring the best results is to have a batter take long practice sessions with a pitcher, hitting only at straight fast balls.

If the swing of your bat is not level, parallel to

The batter holds the bat high as he awaits the ball. He keeps his eyes on the pitcher and the ball at all times. His weight is on the balls of his feet. He shifts the weight to his rear foot. As the ball is thrown, he begins the stride forward by pivoting his shoulders and hips and placing his weight on his front foot. He keeps the bat level as his arms arc through the swing, and snaps his wrists as the bat hits the ball. The swing continues as his body moves into the follow-through.

the ground, you will either miss the pitch, uppercut the ball, pop it up, or bat it into the ground short of the infield. Always follow through with your bat; that is, do not hold back on your swing as soon as you hit the ball. The level swing is always possible if you hold the elbow of the left arm close to your body. Your right arm acts as a guide to keep the bat in a horizontal position, and helps your left arm to pull the bat forward. A left-handed batter uses the reverse directions. Your body must always be held straight, never thrown back, when you prepare to swing.

Do not become a "Nervous Nelly," a batsman that waggles his bat and goes through a lot of false motions as the pitcher gets set to pitch. Acquiring these bad habits will throw you way off-balance. Coaches put great emphasis on the level swing, for it prevents young players from swinging at high pitched balls that come in to the plate shoulder-high or even higher, and which would not be called strikes by the umpire.

Grip your bat firmly, your hands close together. A right-handed hitter keeps his right hand on top of his left hand, and a left-handed hitter just the reverse. You should make it a point to watch the close-ups of the best hitters in the big leagues on the television screen and take note of how they flex their fingers on the handle of the bat as they wait for each pitch. It keeps the muscles of a hitter's arms relaxed, and if you have sharp eyes you will notice that their grip on the bat tightens when they prepare to swing at a pitch.

When you begin to pile up too many strike-outs, try moving your hands a little farther away from the bat handle. You may have to take a shorter swing, but you will find that you have better control of the bat. It is very doubtful that you would profit by choosing a heavier bat, for it would take you a second or two longer bringing your bat around when you take your swing. When you have played long enough and have become an experienced batsman, you will know the right kind of bat to use by the feel of it.

There are four types of batters:

1. The Choke Hitter Such a batsman never gets many extra-base hits, but he generally has a good batting average and seldom strikes out. The bat is held far up on the handle, and the batsman swings at the ball with a short level stroke. The choke hitter as a rule hits to all parts of the diamond and most of the hits are singles that drop just beyond the reach of infielders and outfielders. In baseball jargon he hits them "where they ain't." The greatest choke hitter of all time according to the record books was Willie Keeler of the old Baltimore Orioles.

2. The Pull Hitter. This batsman takes a full swing at the ball and follows through before the pitch is even with his body. He connects with the ball well ahead of his front foot before the ball has passed over any part of the plate. A right-handed hitter pulls the ball to left; the left-handed hitter to right. Outfielders are generally ready for the pull hitters and get the jump on the balls even as they are hit.

3. The Straightaway Hitter He hits the ball where it is pitched, according to the way the pitcher delivers it. A right-handed hitter will hit the inside pitch to the left side of the diamond, and a left-handed hitter to the other side. If the pitcher throws the ball right over the heart of the plate, this type of batsman will hit straightaway to center field. If he gets an outside pitch, he will hit it to that part of the field opposite to his position at the plate.

4. The Slice or Late Hitter He is the hit-and-run batter. He swings late at the ball and hits it into the field opposite his position in the batter's box. To be this type of hitter you have to stand far enough away from the plate so that you won't hit pitches on the inside corner with the handle of your bat. Keep away from the ball, for it is almost impossible to slice an inside pitch with a late swing.

BUNTING This is one of the most important offensive weapons in the game of baseball. It is used to advance a base runner or get a runner on first base when a run is sorely needed. There are two kinds of bunts, the sacrifice bunt and the drag bunt. The sacrifice means that the batsman has given himself up as an out in order to advance a

Larry Brown helps a player perfect the sacrifice bunting position. Holding the bat, you should choke up on it and slide your other hand to the label.

runner or runners on the bases and put them in scoring position. The drag bunt is an attempt at a base hit by the batsman and is always bunted on the ground between the pitcher's mound and first base. This type of bunt has to be made by a fast runner, and a left-handed hitter has the advantage over the right-handed hitter because he is more than a full step closer to first base.

When you are called upon to bunt, an order that you must never ignore, bring your back foot up almost even with your front foot in a comfortable, spread stance and face directly toward the pitcher. Your bat should be absolutely level, parallel to the ground, and held loosely, the upper hand slid up close to the label on the bat, the lower hand on the bat handle. The ball is topped; there is no

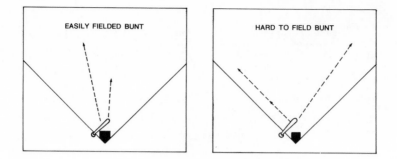

EASILY FIELDED BUNT

HARD TO FIELD BUNT

follow-through. A ball correctly bunted or "laid" down" has very little momentum as it hits the ground. It will not go up into the air.

You should never attempt to bunt any pitches too far out of the strike zone unless you are up at bat on a hit and run squeeze play. In that case you must bunt, for the runner on third is already on his way to the plate. If you let the ball go by, the runner is an easy out. If you foul the pitch off, he can go back to third to wait for your next attempt. If you bunt the ball successfully on the squeeze play, the runner has a great chance to score before the bunt is fielded and thrown into the catcher.

Bunts generally occur when there is a man on first or men on first and second. A sacrifice bunt puts both runners in scoring position. Drag bunts are surprise maneuvers; they should only be attempted when your opponents least expect it. The bunted ball should be placed inside the third or first base line, for one placed out in front of the

114

plate offers an easy play at first for either the pitcher or catcher. If you are fleet of foot and bat left-handed, you should bunt outside pitches toward first base. If you are batting right-handed, bunt the ball in the opposite direction. You will find that if you bunt contrary to these suggestions, you will be completely out of position to start for first base, and in many instances you will pop the ball into the air.

Don't forget. The more firmly you grip the bat, the harder you will bunt the ball. Your bat has to be perfectly controlled, but loosely held. The art of bunting can only be mastered by constant practice and if you become a better than average bunter, you will be as valuable to your team as a home run hitter.

THE BASE PATHS   The instant you hit a pitched ball you become a base runner. You do not have to be exceptionally fast on your feet if you remember to keep your eyes open and your head up when running bases. Run out every hit no matter where it goes, for the best outfielders and infielders are not immune to errors. A fumble or a moment of hesitation on the part of a fielder gives a base runner the chance to make that extra base. Your first objective, of course, is to reach first base safely. Loafing on the way to that base has robbed batters of many base hits. Never assume that a ball you hit directly at or to a fielder is a sure out.

To be a good base runner know the shortest path between bases; they are laid out in the form of a square and you cannot turn sharp right angles at full speed without allowing for the turn. Your approach to a base must be in an arc when you intend to continue on to the next base without breaking stride, and hit the *inside* corner of the bag with whatever foot is in position to make contact, without any false step.

THE PIVOT When you run to first on a base hit or on a fly ball to the outfield, pivot directly around the bag to save time and distance if you attempt to take second base. When you are about four strides away from the base you are rounding, pivot on your right foot; that is, throw your weight heavily on that foot as it hits the ground. Your other foot, hitting the ground, brings your body around in a direct line with the succeeding base because of the movement of that right foot. Your left foot comes in contact with the base. Never shorten your stride before reaching a base, particularly the last few steps. All pivoting should be done at full speed.

THE SLIDE The purpose of the slide is to keep a runner from over-running a base and also to give the baseman as small a part of a runner's body as possible to try and tag. There is a rule in sliding you must never overlook: When you have made up

116

To avoid injury, keep your arms up in the air when you slide.

your mind to slide, *never* change it. Sudden stops and halfway slides can cost you a bad sprain or a broken leg, so avoid that mental lapse. When sliding, always keep both hands in the air to guard against injury to your wrists or fingers.

There are two methods of sliding into bases: head-first and feet-first. Very few coaches recommend the head-first slide, for the risk of injury is great. Only expert base runners use it. Employing the feet-first slide, you throw your body sidewise through the air so that one side of it makes contact with the ground, the weight of your body being on your lower limbs from the hips to the feet. Your lower leg should be bent a little at the knee while the upper foot hooks the bag. This is why it is called the hook slide. Be careful, however, that the

117

The hook slide should be practiced carefully.

spikes of the shoe of your lower foot do not catch in the dirt. It could mean a broken bone.

Always avoid the straight-in slide, that is, going into a base with both feet close together. The spikes of one or both shoes could catch on the ground with serious results.

Timing a slide is of great importance. Your slide should not start too soon or too late. It all depends upon how quick a ball is being thrown to the base you are trying to reach or how accurate the throw is. If you slide late. you will most likely over-slide the bag, and if too soon, you will fail to reach the base and be easily tagged out.

When you are about to slide, try to keep your eyes on the man guarding the base and if possible the flight of the ball thrown into the baseman. If he comes forward for a thrown ball, slide in on the right side of your body to the outside of the diamond, and hook the base with your left foot. If the baseman has to go back a few steps for the ball, slide to the inside of the diamond and hook the bag with your right foot.

STEALING BASES You do not always need a big lead off first base to steal off an opposing pitcher. Bear in mind, too, that a runner never steals off the catcher. If you have the ability to make a quick start, you have about all the qualifications you need to be a good base stealer. And if you keep the following procedures always in your mind:

1. Stay on the bag at first base until you are sure that the pitcher has the ball and that the pitcher is in his correct position on the pitching plate. If he is on the pitching rubber without the ball, a balk will be called against him.

2. As soon as the pitcher comes into his pitching position, take your lead off the bag, but do not make your lead so great that it will prevent you from getting back to the bag in case the pitcher tries to pick you off.

3. Keep the weight of your body well distributed on both feet so that you have good body control.

4. A safe lead is usually two steps and a slide away from the bag.

The base runner takes a lead off first, ready to steal.

5. Be sure to watch left-handed pitchers very closely. They use the same body and leg movements pitching to a batter as they do when throwing to first base. Their throwing hand is much closer to first base than those of right-handed pitchers, and the pick-off throws get to first base more quickly.

6. Make a study of the habits and peculiarities of the opposing pitchers when you are sitting on the bench between innings. Mentally jot them down so that you will know which pitchers are easy to steal on and which are not. Notice that there is a difference between the pitcher's knee action on a throw to the batter and on a throw to first base, and a difference in movement of the pitcher's foot.

There are three types of steals starting at first base. First is the plain steal, getting a good jump on the pitcher to get to second base in scoring position. This is the steal most often attempted. The success of the second type of steal, delayed steal, depends upon the alertness of the catcher, the shortstop, and the second baseman. If a catcher has the bad habit of lobbing the ball back to the pitcher, you, the base runner, should make a quick dash for second the moment the ball leaves the catcher's hand. Even though the catcher sees you break for second and checks his toss back to the pitcher, he is bound to lose precious seconds in assuming his correct throwing position. His throw is often hurried and goes wild.

If the second baseman or shortstop fail to move toward second after each pitch, they will have to take the catcher's throw on the run and will be out of position in trying to make the tag on the runner going into second base.

Third is the double steal, which is used mostly when there are runners on first and third with fewer than two outs. If you are the runner on third, do not take too big a lead off the bag for a snap throw to third by the catcher could put you out. Do not try to score before the catcher makes his throw to second to try and cut down that runner attempting to steal second. That runner often stops between bases and makes a move back to first to get himself into a run-up play, giving you a chance to try and score from third. If you are caught in a run-up play between third and home plate, then the runner on first has a great chance of getting to second, in scoring position. Again, this play's success depends largely upon a lack of awareness on the part of the opponent's second baseman and shortstop, when they fail to take those steps toward second base to cover, with each pitched ball.

BASE RUNNING RULES TO REMEMBER

1. Make every effort to get to third base when there is only one man out, but do not take that chance when no one is out or when two men are out.

2. When you are a base runner on first and a ball is hit to the outfield, you should look at the ball as it is fielded, just before you reach second base. If you catch the outfielder in a non-throwing position, try for the extra base.

3. If you are a runner on second and a ball is hit to third base, you should make every attempt to reach that base on the third baseman's throw to first for the out on the batsman.

4. When you are a runner on any base and a long hit goes to the outfield, you have a chance to advance a base if the ball is caught; that is, if you have not taken too long a lead off that base. You would have to go back to that base and tag it with your foot before trying to advance to the next base.

5. Know the infield fly rule. If, before two men are out, and runners are on bases, a batsman hits a fair fly ball an infielder can handle easily, he is automatically out. If you are a base runner, you

A demonstration of the lead and posture from second base.

advance at your own risk. A bunted ball popped up to the infield is not regarded as an infield fly.

6. Stealing home is a desperation play and is never attempted under ordinary conditions. Facing a certain situation your coach or manager might signal to you to make the attempt, if it is the last inning of a ball game and your team needs a run to tie or go ahead, and two men are out. Your chances to score rest upon your speed, the length of the lead you have taken off third, and whether the pitcher takes a full wind-up. The pitcher's quick throw could be wild enough to make it impossible for the catcher to tag you out at the plate. It goes without saying that you will have to make a long slide when stealing home and might find yourself

123

blocked off the plate. Steals of home are few indeed.

Put yourself in the hands of the third base coach when you are a runner at that base or are running toward that base from second. Your back is to the defensive play and the third base coach will tell you to slide or not to slide. He will tell you the number of outs made and any situation that is expected to develop. In case a ball is hit to the outfield the coach will hold you to the bag until the ball is caught or goes for a base hit. On a hit to the infield you should make no move if he holds his arms high. If he waves them toward the plate, you make the attempt to score.

If you're a runner on first, the coach there will alert you to the play to expect and the number of outs. He will let you know whether or not you can reach second base on a wild throw to first, and he will watch the moves of the first baseman to guard against a throw from either the pitcher or catcher that might pick you off.

CHAPTER TWELVE

CONDITIONING AND PRACTICE

If you want to succeed in baseball, you must bring your body to its highest state of physical development. Whether you succeed or not might be related to the following five rules:

1. Abstain from alcoholic beverages and drugs.

2. Do not use tobacco in any form.

3. Refrain from overeating at any time.

4. Get nine hours of sleep every day.

5. Eat good, wholesome food.

Setting up exercises before the baseball season begins will trim you down to your correct weight according to your height. Knee bends, sit-ups, trunk twisters, and other basic exercises will help keep you in shape.

It is also essential that you do plenty of running to develop your leg muscles and breathing, and if you are an infielder or outfielder get in a lot of throwing, though not enough to put a strain on your arm muscles.

Avoid unnecessary injuries. Never wear a ring on your finger during the course of a ball game, and do not forget to keep your fingernails cut short at all times. Nail injuries often take several weeks to heal completely.

Loosen up by playing catch or with a pepper game. This is either a group of players arranged in a circle throwing the ball to each other to improve their efficiency with the glove or it is a batsman hitting short ground balls or pop-ups to a group of players, in close, with a wooden or wire fence acting as a backstop. The pitcher should warm up to throw batting practice, and as soon as he is ready start real practice. He should throw to the batters for fifteen minutes, then get relief. The pitcher should concentrate on getting the ball over the plate for the batter and to perfect his own control. He should change his pitching position on the rubber, winding up to throw to one batter, holding a man on base when the next batter comes up.

The major portion of a two-hour practice session should be confined to hitting, and the players should know their turns at bat by a list made out by either a supervisor, coach, or manager. No more than two players should be near the plate awaiting their turn at bat. All other players should go to their positions in the field. "Bunt one and hit three," is usually the order of the man in charge of the workout. He will expect you to run out your last hit as fast as you possibly can, then slow up and stop after making the wide turn at first base.

Play each ball on the defensive as if you were in a real ball game. Second basemen and short-stops should constantly practice handling hard-hit ground balls and making pivots. Use two players, one on the left field foul line near the plate, the other on the right field line, one hitting fungoes to the outfielders, the other hitting grounders to the infield. The outfielders should work on making throws to second base, third base, and to home plate, always remembering to throw at a cutoff man who should be in his correct position.

The last fifteen minutes of practice should be devoted to individual or team weaknesses spotted by the coaches during the last competitive game played. These include pitching, fielding bunts, base running, and batting.

THE COACH When do you try to steal the next base? When do you bunt? How do you know if the hit-and-run play is on? Look to your coach for those signals, for even the most experienced ball players are not expected to predetermine every offensive tactic in a ball game. Signals should be as simple and as few as possible; too many can be confusing. Most of them can be flashed by altering movements of the body, and they must be plainly seen by batsmen and base runners.

All members of a squad should memorize the coaches' signals, which of course are changed from time to time lest they be "read" by the opposing team. A base runner leading off second base has a clear view of the opponents' catcher and he is considered the best signal "stealer."

At times, in order to confuse the other team a coach will let someone other than himself flash the signals, but this is a procedure not recommended below big league level. The responsibility for the success of a given play put on a youngster's shoulders could have an adverse affect on his mental attitude.

A young person who participates in the game of baseball benefits mentally as well as physically. He is taught to be considerate of others no matter what their race, color, or creed may be. He is taught the meaning of sacrifice and not just when he is up to bat to lay down a bunt. Whether he becomes a professional ball player or not, he has absorbed the principles of fair play, honesty, and loyalty.

If you have carefully studied this book, you should have acquired a thorough knowledge of how the game of baseball is played. An apprentice in any line of endeavor must have the patience and desire to succeed. Only constant practice combined with a healthy mind and body and full confidence in yourself can lift you to the stature of a big league ball player. It is entirely up to you.